THE
DISTINGUISHING
MARK OF
LEADERSHIP

THE
DISTINGUISHING
MARK OF
LEADERSHIP

DON MEYER

MORNING JOY MEDIA
Spring City, Pennsylvania

Published by Morning Joy Media.

Visit www.morningjoymedia.com for more information on bulk discounts and special promotions, or e-mail your questions to info@morningjoymedia.com.

Cover Design: Doug Smith
Author Photo: Hoffer Photography
Interior Design: Debbie Capeci
Journey Inward & Journey Outward graphics: Chris Jones

Subject Headings:

1. Leadership—Religious aspects—Christianity. 2. Leadership—Biblical teaching. 3. Christian life. I. Title.

ISBN 978-1-937107-45-1 (paperback)
ISBN 978-1-937107-46-8 (ebook)

Printed in the United States of America

To my loving wife and best friend, Evie—
The keeper of my heart
The joy in my life
The inspiration to my mind
The encourager on my spiritual journey
ALWAYS!

CONTENTS

PART III: THE LEGACY QUESTION

Chapter 10
How Do I Want to Be Remembered on Earth
and Received in Heaven? • 219

CONCLUSION

FOREWORD

Every time I'm around Don Meyer I learn something new, which is a high compliment. And it's one reason I like being around him. Another is that Don Meyer is as gracious as they come. Our friendship spans more than a decade, and I've been the beneficiary of his grace and wisdom.

Thousands of books have been written to help make us better leaders, but I'm biased toward books by authors that I know and trust. While I have an entrepreneurial streak that craves "the latest and greatest" ideas, my greatest respect is reserved for those who have "been there and done that"—who have a proven track record of long obedience in the same direction. That's Don Meyer.

Don says in this book that it's not only important to encounter leadership ideas as we read, but we must also find ways to integrate those ideas into our lives. A downpour of 12 inches of rain will only be of help if it soaks into the soil. If it falls on an impervious parking lot, it will just run off into a drain.

Don suggests that the way we soak in leadership ideas is through asking leadership questions. It is why he says, "The most important mark of leadership is the question mark."

With models from antiquity, including Jesus and Socrates, Don has brought here a methodology which can transform your leadership journey. Leadership questions will build a bridge between new ideas and how they apply to us. Our questions will make us think and ponder and pray. If we are honest with ourselves, our questions will change us.

Don does not claim to identify all of the questions we as leaders should ask, but he does provide ten important questions every leader will want to ask. Within these questions are examples of the way he has applied them to his own life and ministry. It is in these practical examples that he reminds us that no matter how long we are on our leadership journey, there are always new things to learn and better ways to do things. In a nutshell, keep asking questions!

Leadership questions can function as a mirror for us to take internal inventory of where we are. Leadership questions can also function as a window to look outside of ourselves to see all the potential of what we might become.

As you read this book, these questions will help you become a better leader!

—MARK BATTERSON

Lead Pastor, National Community Church,
Washington, DC, and bestselling author

PREFACE

WHAT IS THE SYMBOL ON THE COVER
AND WHY WAS IT CHOSEN?

The symbol on the cover is called an ***interrobang***. An interrobang (a.k.a. *interabang*, and pronounced *in-ter-uh-bang*) is informally known as a *quexclamation mark*, a nonstandard symbol used in various written languages to combine the functions of the question mark (interrogation point) and the exclamation mark (exclamation point). A sentence ending with an interrobang asks a question in an excited (with passion) manner, expresses excitement or disbelief in the form of a question, or asks a rhetorical question.

As you will see in this book, questions have enormously influenced my private and public life. And though I started out with a large question mark on the cover, as I wrote the book I realized that the impact of these questions on my life and leadership was much greater than a mere question mark could capture. For me, these are passionate, dynamic, inspiring, challenging, never-be-the-same questions that transform everything in my life. They had an impact on my life and leadership like questions on steroids.

I would invite you, then, to read the questions in this book with that same fervent, white-hot passion.

INTRODUCTION

*If I were an enemy of a movement, I would get its
leaders obsessed with the wrong questions.*
Reggie McNeal

Sometimes questions are more important than answers.
Nancy Willard

*Oh my soul... Be prepared for him who
knows how to ask questions.*
T. S. Elliot

I will never forget the day we visited the fourteenth-cen-
tury cathedral in Nantwich, England. We were returning
by train from the Hill Country with two couples who, on a
whim, decided to visit their friends in that old British town
of fourteen thousand people. Located in the center of town,
St. Mary's Church is considered one of the finest medieval
churches in all of England. And they just had to show it to us.

Built of red sandstone, this cathedral is an architectural
treasure. Once inside, our eyes adjusted to the light. Our guide
pointed out the spectacular stained glass windows, the huge
canopies, and the complexity of detail in the medieval wood
carvings, considered the finest in the country.

But the massive pillars supporting the entire structure were
what caught my attention. At first, they resembled the pillars
of any cathedral, but as our guide told us to look closer, we

saw an unusual feature. If he had not pointed it out to us, we never would have seen it.

Where one section of a stone pillar rested on the next one, a small, clear glass plate was attached by two screws, with one in each section. The purpose of this glass plate was to signal any compromise in the foundation. Even the slightest shift would break the glass, allowing authorities to take corrective measures before catastrophic problems arose. They called these glass plates "telltales" because they "told the tale" of the architecture.

Our guide then pointed out many of them at different places on all of the pillars. I couldn't help but imagine how tragic it would be if those plates were made of an elastic substance. By the time someone responded to the seismic shifts, the whole structure could be compromised and perhaps even collapse.

Years ago, my friend Dr. Dan Mortensen asked me to present a workshop on leadership to a group of newly chosen student leaders at the University of Valley Forge (I was invited to serve as the president of Valley Forge Christian College on January 1, 1997. On September 16, 2014, VFCC became the University of Valley Forge. I'll use University of Valley Forge [UVF] throughout this book). As I prepared my presentation, I pondered my own leadership journey. How did I change over the years? What processes have I gone through (and still go through) to improve as a leader? How have the organizations to which I have belonged changed over the years, requiring me to change my leadership style?

As I thought about those questions, I made a critical discovery: Constantly asking myself leadership questions is standard practice for me. I remember as a young pastor asking myself, *What does it mean to be a pastor?* For seven years I kept asking that question, and for seven years the answer kept changing because I kept changing and the church kept changing.

After graduate school, I was invited to serve as a professor at North Central University (formerly North Central Bible College). My question changed to *What does it mean to be a professor?* If my classes were too easy or too difficult, my students would be easily discouraged on their academic journeys, which would mean I was failing to be an excellent professor.

After three years, I was invited to serve as the academic dean and later the vice president of academic affairs. For the next eighteen years I kept asking, *What does it mean to be in administrative ministry in that role?* Over those years the institution kept changing and I kept changing, requiring me to keep asking that question again and again.

Although this is a book on leadership, I also find myself asking questions on a personal level. *What does it mean for me to be Evie's husband?* The answer is obviously quite different today than when we were first married in 1967.

As our sons, Darin and Kevin, were growing up, *What does it mean for me to be their father?* took on different realities before first grade and in these many years since high school and college. When Noah, our grandson, came along, I began asking a new question: *What does it mean to be a grandfather* (or *Poppy,* as Noah calls me)?

This methodology of asking questions has merged into every public and private dimension of my life. Even my walk with God was affected as I asked the question, *What does it mean to be a follower of Jesus?*

I cannot overstate how important this methodology has been in my life. Literally, I find myself asking all kinds of questions every day. Any routine initiative is loaded with new questions. Any new initiative is loaded with new questions.

In his classic book *The Art Spirit*, Robert Henri boldly claims, "All education is self-education."[1] Although Henri's truism applies to education, it could also apply to the personal responsibility each of us has in public and private life. If we are functioning poorly, we can't blame our families or our culture or our organizations. It's our personal responsibility. Our questions compel us to own every part of our leadership journey.

Which brings me to the heart of this book: I suggest that *the distinguishing mark of leadership is the question mark.* The questions we ask about the quality of our leadership will function like those telltales in that old Nantwich cathedral. They will compel us to keep checking on the entire infra-structure of our leadership. And, if the "glass breaks," they will challenge us to take immediate corrective measure.

The interrobang on the cover of this book (the question mark intertwined with the exclamation point) illustrates graphically the ultimate goal of any leader, particularly a Christian leader. Asking distinctive and insightful questions will always enhance our leadership. This process of asking questions and then living out the answers will make our leadership pleasing to God who, when it is all said and done, will give us the ultimate exclamation point with his words, "Well done, good and faithful servant."

Come with me as we ponder together this distinguishing mark of leadership—**the question mark**.

WHY WRITE ANOTHER BOOK ON LEADERSHIP?

You may wonder why anyone would want to write another book on leadership. Are not our shelves full enough with the insights of leadership specialists like Warren Bennis, Peter Drucker, John Kotter, Ken Blanchard, John Maxwell, Max Dupree, Bob Rhoden, Steven Covey, Ed Berkey, Tom Peters, Malcolm Gladwell and Lee Bolman, to name a few? I love these books. My books are my friends. I will keep acquiring them and reading them.

But, in order to be an effective leader, one must do more than just read books. There must be a process of integrating their insights into our own leadership journey. I have often taken notes at the seminars leaders have taught, or I have placed comments in the margins of their books, only to find myself putting my notes in a file and placing the books back on my shelves. The ideas inspired and informed me for a season but too rarely did they change me.

That's why the question mark is such an important mark in leadership. Our questions will help challenge our current thinking. Our questions will form a bridge between a new idea and how it applies to us. Our questions will help us to be honest with ourselves. Our questions will distinguish us, set us apart, and define us as leaders.

THE METHODOLOGY OF ASKING QUESTIONS

An Answer from Antiquity. Socrates, the fifth-century philosopher, said, "The unexamined life is not worth living." And although he wrote nothing, his students (especially Plato and Xenophon) captured both his thoughts and methodology, which is known as the Socratic Method.

Socrates was an expert at asking questions. His dialogues probe deeply into the pursuit of truth. His original hearers, as well as readers today, wrestle with the answers. They force us to examine our lives.

Socrates modeled for us this timeless and probing methodology of asking questions. Of course, he demonstrated that few questions are entirely objective. As a philosopher and keen thinker, he often injected his own theories into his dialogues. From him we also learn that even the best methodologies have limitations.

An Answer from the Bible. While reading through the Bible several years ago, I couldn't help but notice the questions that were asked. I decided to count them and I found just over two thousand, five hundred questions.

Some of the biblical questions are found in the routine narrative of everyday life, with significance going hardly beyond the moment. For example, Philip asked, "Do you understand what you are reading?" (Acts 8:30) or Paul asked, "What do you prefer?" (1 Cor. 4:21). These kinds of questions are simply a part of normal, everyday exchange.

Other questions, however, probe to the very soul of the individual. God's questions are like that. Consider God's question to Adam, "Where are you?" (Gen. 3:9). It was obvious they were not playing hide and seek and at that point God couldn't find Adam. God knew exactly where Adam was, but he wanted *Adam* to know where Adam was. The question exposed Adam's disobedience.

Or consider the question when God asked Jonah, "Is it right for you to be angry?" (Jonah 4:4). Earlier Jonah had refused to obey God, who told him to go to preach to Nineveh, Israel's bitter enemy. After his deep-sea repentance, Jonah went to Nineveh, and after his sermon the city repented and the judgment of God was thwarted. But when Jonah thought about Nineveh's escape from judgment, and then on top of that lost his air conditioning, he became very angry. The question God asked of Jonah exposed Jonah's selfish values for himself and also for his people, Israel.

Jesus used this methodology with laser precision. A study of Jesus' questions reveals a master teacher at work. Whether he was asking a blind man, "Do you believe that I am able to do this?" (Matt. 9:28) or the Pharisees, "And if I drive out demons by Beelzebub, by whom do your people drive them out?" (Matt. 12:27), Jesus knew how to expose the conditions of the heart through his questions.

His disciples were challenged again and again by his questions. When he asked, "Who do people say the Son of Man is?" (Matt. 16:13) or "But what about you?…Who do you say I am?" (Matt. 16:15), he was probing the depths of their perception of him.

It was impossible for the people who encountered the questions of Jesus to avoid dealing with their true feelings.

Questions compel us to internalize the issues. They force us to ask, *So what?* They move us from theory to reality. They help us discover reality, but, more than that, they help us own the process.

THE IMPORTANCE OF HONESTY

For this methodology to work, however, I cannot overemphasize the importance of honesty. As Robertson McQuilken wisely said, "It is impossible for me to help a dishonest man." Leadership questions only help us if we are honest with ourselves and with our answers. When the doctor asks us a health question, we can only receive help to the degree that we are honest.

Asking meaningless questions will certainly not help us. But asking important questions and then giving dishonest answers will ultimately harm us.

THE PROBING QUESTIONS

I would invite you to step inside a very different kind of leadership book. In this book you will not be challenged to find all the answers to your leadership questions. Nor will you be asked all the questions which can be asked about your leadership. But if you can learn this *methodology*, you will continue to discover for the rest of your life why the question mark could be the distinguishing mark of leadership for you as a leader.

Whether you're a beginner or veteran, join me in considering some of the most important questions that I have asked myself on my leadership journey over the years. Of course, this process must never end.

After you have walked with me though the questions that guided me, I encourage you to prepare your own list of leadership questions and keep asking them over and over. The challenging questions we will be asking fall into three categories.

PART I: THE LOFTY QUESTION

Chapter 1. *What Does It Mean to Be a Follower of Jesus?* Christian leaders must first ask this question. It profoundly affects everything. How does my relationship with Jesus influence me as a leader and how I lead? Without a doubt, this is the most important question of all. Am I prepared to follow Jesus and do all he expects in every dimension of my leadership quest? What exactly does that mean? What might be the cost? Is my relationship with him lukewarm or white hot? This we will not be able to camouflage. As the jazz musician Charlie Porter said, "If it ain't in your heart, it ain't in your horn."

PART II: THE LIFE QUESTIONS

Chapter 2. *What Is the Culture/Spirit of the Organization?* Our leadership style must fit with the culture and spirit of the organization we are trying to lead. If everyone around me is going north and south and I am going east and west, something is wrong. Is it my responsibility to adapt to the organization or to have the organization adapt to me?

Chapter 3. *What Is Expected of Me?* I once heard that everyone has an agenda for the leader. Rarely does the phone ring or the email message arrive just because someone wants to share a compliment. Expectations come at us from all directions. One of my mentors once said, "There are a lot of things that need to be done in the world, but you can't do them all." From our job description to the Christian graces with which we carry it out, what expectations should receive our primary attention?

Chapter 4. *How Do I Lead with Vision?* Harry Emerson Fosdick said, "Eyes that look are common; eyes that see are rare." One of the qualities of the ancient Hebrew prophet is embedded in the term *seer*. These anointed leaders had a heightened capacity to see what others could not see. Effective leaders must have vision or they will never be great leaders.

Chapter 5. *What Does It Mean to Follow/Lead and to Lead/ Follow?* Just about every book on leadership addresses the subject of followership. You can't lead effectively unless you know how to follow. But what does it mean to follow? You may need to learn how to follow before you lead. You will need to continue to follow as you continue to lead. What about loyalty? Do you blindly follow?

Chapter 6. *How Do I Effectively Manage My Time?* We all know our lives are busy, often too busy. When I ponder the role of Sabbath in my life I usually feel more guilt than encouragement. I must confess that the older I get the easier it is to say no to certain demands, but I still find my watch moving too fast and my work moving too slow. Can I find a solution that will help me look back on my life without regret?

Chapter 7. *How Do I Balance My Public Life and My Private Life?* A. W. Tozer said, "Truth is like a bird. It cannot fly with one wing. Yet we are forever trying to take off with one wing flapping furiously while the other is tucked neatly out of sight." The tug of war between our public life and our private life is relentless. How do we keep it in balance?

Chapter 8. *How Do I Keep Growing as a Leader?* How sad it would be if a student peaked at graduation. Or what if that first year out of college were lived over and over again, year after year, for the next twenty years? Morton Kelsey speaks of "the questing spirit." Do I have an insatiable quest to keep growing in every area of my life, specifically as a leader?

Chapter 9. *Why Does God Allow Me to Go Through Adversity?* Sooner or later, every Christian leader will face adversity. Some storms are mere cloudbursts and all we need is an umbrella. Others take us out at the knees. The question we will ask early and often will be the *Why* question. When the temperature goes down and the paper work piles up, unless we settle that question in our hearts, our faith will falter and our future will be clouded.

PART III: THE LEGACY QUESTION

Chapter 10. *How Will I Be Remembered on Earth and Received in Heaven?* What kind of legacy do I want to leave on earth? The first legacy I think of relates to my personal life. What kind of legacy do I want to leave with my family? We all know that the greatest legacy is not the size of the inheritance we leave behind. But what do we want to leave them?

Then there is the public side of my legacy. Perhaps, if we have an impressive résumé or if our organization grows to a certain size or if we have attained economic sustainability or if our reputation exceeds our press releases, then we'll know we have left a great legacy. Perhaps it's a name on a building or song or book that will finally assuage the longing in our heart to do something that will last after we are gone. Someone said, "Do you really want to have a funeral that no one attends other than for business reasons?"

The second part of the legacy question is, *How will I be received in heaven?* There is an eternal dimension to the legacy question. At the end of it all, no other question really matters. How tragic it would be if we met everyone else's expectations of us but missed this one. What if we "gained the whole world and then lost our own soul." What a tragedy indeed.

In his *The 7 Habits of Highly Effective People*, Steven Covey's second habit is "Begin with the End in Mind."[2] One day all of our leadership responsibilities will end. The calendar always wins. What will ultimately matter?

It takes an enormous amount of courage to ask these probing questions. I trust you're beginning to understand why the distinguishing mark of leadership is the question mark. Good questions asked and answered well will always make you a better and more effective leader. And that will result in the final exclamation point on our life when God says, "Well done, good and faithful servant." I'm sure the life mission statements for all of us have that as our ultimate goal.

MY POINT OF VIEW

During his message in a UVF chapel, Dr. Peter Kuzmic said, "One's point of view is always from one's view of a point." To illustrate his idea, he had us extend our arm, point our thumb to the ceiling and look past our thumb to an object on the wall in front of us. He then told us to close one eye and observe what we saw and then close the other eye and observe what we saw. We immediately understood him. One's point of view is always from one's own individual view of a point.

This book reflects my point of view. Over the years, the places where I have ministered and the people with whom I have ministered, the lessons I have learned and the books I have read have all contributed to the life context from which I write. Therefore, many of the examples and illustrations used in this book are taken from that context.

Ladies and gentlemen—let the questions begin!

PART I

The Lofty Question

CHAPTER 1

What Does It Mean to Be a Follower of Jesus?

Christianity has not so much been tried and found wanting as it has been found difficult and left untried.
G. K. Chesterton

When Christ calls a man, he bids him come and die.
Dietrich Bonhoeffer

If you seek God, the answers will find you.
Mark Batterson

Dr. Gordon Fee surprised me when he began his presentation with these words, "The longer I live the more I keep asking myself, *What does it mean to be a Christian?*" It seemed like such an elementary question for this world-class New Testament scholar to ask. The answer seemed obvious to me. Or was it? He repeated it several times and the more he repeated it, the more I doubted my first reaction.

As he continued, I realized he was going deep into the heart of the gospel by identifying the linchpin of what it means to follow Jesus. The Bible clearly teaches that we become Christians the moment we invite Jesus into our life; becoming like Jesus in our character, however, takes place throughout an entire lifetime. That question means more than it might first appear.

That question and the way we answer it will seep into every part of our lives. It will affect every motive behind every action. It will dominate everything from the moment we hear our alarm in the morning until we set it at night. It will peek around every corner. We will hear it in every song. We will see it in every relationship. Nothing will be exempt.

We can sense it in Jesus' question, "Who do you say I am?" (Matt. 16:15). And when Peter answered "You are the Messiah, the Son of the living God," Jesus then said, "Blessed are you, Simon son of Jonah, for this was not revealed to you by flesh and blood, but by my Father in heaven" (Matt. 16:16–17). Peter knew that Jesus was, in the words of Josh McDowell, "more than a carpenter."

The Christian leader must ask this question first and foremost: *What does it mean to follow Jesus?* If we get this question wrong, everything else will go wrong. To get this question right means the very foundation of every leadership initiative we will ever take will have the potential of being right.

THE COST OF FOLLOWING JESUS

In Luke 14:25–33, Jesus presented an invitation to follow him in spite of the cost. Large crowds were already following him. He could have done something spectacular to garner more attention and to get even more to join. But instead, he placed before everyone this huge challenge. He spoke of counting the cost before you build a tower or battle an enemy. You just don't wake up one morning and begin something without taking an inventory of what you are going to face. No one does that.

And, if you are going to follow Jesus as a Christian leader, you must count the cost. Dietrich Bonhoeffer said, "When Christ calls a man, he bids him come and die."[1] The cost of being a follower of Jesus may be greater than anything you could ever imagine.

Crowds gathered around him until then, but, according to John 6:66, many went back and walked no more with him when they saw that following him was not popular. The price was too difficult and they didn't want to pay it. No wonder the poet Browning said, "How very hard it is to be a Christian, hard for you and me."

This seems like a strange method. It almost sounds like Jesus is trying to discourage people from following him. But rather than present only the joys and thrills and adventures of following him, Jesus was honest. He didn't pull a bait-and-switch ploy on them.

Why would he do it that way? He was looking for men and women of quality. The crowds were there but he wanted more than just lots of people. He knew that when they were building the church and battling the enemy, he needed people who could stand when the going got tough.

To be a genuine follower, Jesus gave these three non-negotiable conditions.

WE MUST GIVE OUR LOVE

Luke 14:26, "If anyone comes to me and does not hate father and mother, wife and children, brothers and sisters—yes, even their own life—such a person cannot be my disciple."

Does that mean we should all gather our family around us and declare to them, "I hate you"? Obviously not. This passage includes what scholars call "the language of exaggerated contrast." Our love for our families—which must be genuine and selfless—must, in comparison to our love for God, be as hate.

If we are true followers of Jesus, then he can have no other rivals in our lives. The first commandment expects that we have "no other gods" before Jehovah God. For Israel, they were called upon to sacrifice the firstborn of their flock to God as a way of demonstrating this priority. They had no idea if another animal would be born. God wanted from them the first and the best.

God instituted the tithe for the very same reason. He wants to be first. God does not want the change in the bottom of our pockets, the leftovers after we have used our money on ourselves. As someone said, "The gift without the giver is bare." God was saying to Israel, "I want you more than I want your stuff."

Ask any woman what she would rather have—a gift of two dozen roses from someone who doesn't love her or a handful of dandelions scooped up and given by a grateful child saying, "I sure do love you, Mommy." Perhaps some would prefer the roses, but I think most would take the dandelions any day.

I must confess, though, that I am not sure I understand the depth of this kind of love. Evie and I were married on August 5, 1967. You do the math. We have shared more than twice as many years together than we did apart. And our love today is deeper than it ever was when we started out together as *we*. Our favorite Browning poem, "Grow old along with me; the best is yet to be; the last of life for which the first was made," says it all.

According to this call to be a follower of Jesus, however, my love for her must be as hate in comparison to my love for God. But I am still learning how to love God with a love which makes that love look like hate.

When God blessed us with our sons, Darin (in 1969) and Kevin (in 1971), our love took on new dimensions. Our love for each other as husband and wife did not decrease; it expanded to include both of them. And for more than four decades we have grown to love them even more. But I'm still learning how to love God with a love which makes that love look like hate.

Then in February of 2003, Noah Ethan Meyer, our first and only grandson, was born. He arrived ten weeks early and had to be in the hospital for several weeks before he could go home. But, the moment we saw him, our love expanded to include him. And when we held him for the first time, we felt as though we had known him and loved him all our lives. Over these years our love for him has grown and grown. I'm sure he is the best grandson in the whole world. (Smile.) But I am still learning how to love God with a love which makes that love look like hate.

For a true follower of Jesus, every other rival must be set aside. He wants the height and depth and breadth and length of our love.

That is the cost of following Jesus. He wants that quality of our love.

WE MUST TAKE UP OUR CROSS

Luke 14:27, "And whoever does not carry their cross and follow me cannot be my disciple."

Crosses mean different things to different people. For some, a cross is a mere decorative piece of jewelry. For others, it is used in a ritual you enact around the Easter season. For others, it may signify ill health or an ill temperament. Someone said, "My sharp tongue is my cross," to which someone else replied, "No, that's not your cross; that's my cross."

For Jesus, the cross meant a voluntary commitment, suffering, sacrifice, and death. He was "despised and rejected of men." They hated him. He was repulsive to them. They would not let him rule over them. But in spite of all that rejection, his love compelled him to willingly wrap his arms around the cross. Anyone who follows Jesus must be willing to take up his cross. It means we must be willing to die to all that displeases him. Lee Maxwell wrote a book titled *Born Crucified*, which highlights the meaning for the follower of Jesus to say with the apostle Paul:

> *I have been crucified with Christ and I no longer live,*
> *but Christ lives in me. The life I now live in the body, I*

live by faith in the Son of God, who loved me and gave
himself for me (Gal. 2:20).

We need a resurrection of the crucified life. What does
it mean to take up our cross? What does it mean to die to
all else that would call for our affection? Unfortunately, our
understanding may resemble the teenager who said, "I'm
not sure if I ever died to self, but I did feel a little faint once."

Dallas Willard said, "The greatest danger to the church
today is that of pitching its message too low." A West Point
dormitory sign says, "The more you sweat in peace, the less
you will bleed in war." Following Jesus is costly for those who
will battle the enemy and build the church.

Don't be discouraged if your Christianity costs you something. Rather, be surprised if it doesn't. In his book *Jesus
Manifesto*, Leonard Sweet's words challenge any Jesus follower, "Two words one would never think of applying to
Jesus of the Gospels: boring and predictable. How is it that
the church has tamed such a character—in Dorothy Sayers'
words 'very efficiently pared the claws of the Lion of Judah
and certified him as a fitting household pet for pale curates
and pious old ladies.'"

Sweet continues, "We have been handed a shrink-wrapped
Jesus, a once a week mascot."[2]

I will never forget my first trip to Israel. The year was 1979.
We planned that trip for two years. One other couple joined
Evie and me as the leaders of thirty college students. I was
teaching a college-level Bible Geography course. I eagerly
anticipated being in the land of the Bible, my first time out
of the country—my first time in Israel. I could hardly wait.

The day of our trip arrived and after a long flight we landed in Amman, Jordan. The following day we went by bus and later horseback to visit the rock-fortressed city of Petra. I will never forget the horseback ride through the narrow path into that ancient city. After all those years, my pictures bring back the desert heat and smells and feelings of that experience.

We returned to our hotel in Amman exhausted, but it was a *good* tired. The next day we crossed over the Jordan River on the Allenby Bridge. At last we were in the land of Israel. Only the prominent Israeli military presence kept me from kissing the ground.

On Monday we were to begin a walking tour of the Old City of Jerusalem. Finally, my paper maps were going to come alive. Finally, I was going to see firsthand those places I had only seen in textbooks. My excitement was at an all-time high.

Early Monday morning I woke up with a stabbing pain in my lower back. At first I thought I pulled muscle, but I soon experienced pain like never before. A few hours later a doctor informed me that I was having a kidney stone attack. They say pain from a kidney stone is worse than the pain of childbirth. I don't know if that is true, but I do know it ground my life to a halt.

Rather than admitting me to a hospital, the doctors gave strong pain medication to help me pass the kidney stone. Monday passed but the stone did not. By Tuesday my eyes were blurring from the medication. Wednesday came and went. Then Thursday and still I had no relief. On Friday, the day our group went north to Galilee, I was admitted into the Hadassah Hospital on Mount Scopus, Jerusalem. As you can imagine, I was not very happy. And I was still in pain.

In the hospital I was hooked up to an IV and finally my eyesight cleared. I opened my Bible to Luke 14 and this text: "And anyone who does not follow me and take up his cross cannot be my disciple." As I reread those words, I sensed God speak to my heart, "What if I called you to serve as a missionary here in Israel? Would you be willing to go?"

Let me share some context. I grew up in a Christian home and sensed a call to ministry after my father died when I was in high school. God used that family loss to redirect my entire life. Prior to that, dairy farming was my career goal. That was all I knew. I had joined the Future Farmers of America (FFA), anticipating a similar career as my father and his father.

But through that experience God called me into the ministry. Also, God used the missionary stories of Jim Elliot and his four friends who were martyred by the Auca Indians in Ecuador to move my heart toward a willingness to place my life on the altar for whatever God had for me.

Over the years, that call from God had taken me to college, pastoral ministry, graduate school, teaching as a professor at North Central University, and administrative ministry as an academic dean. At no time had I ever said no to God's direction or redirection of my life. I know how imperfect I am and how inadequate I felt, but I had always been willing to go wherever God directed me.

But there, in that Israeli hospital bed, I mustered up every bit of my will and with every part of me for the first time in my life I said an emphatic "No." I wanted out of that Middle Eastern hospital where too few people spoke English and the military stood guard. I wanted to go back home as soon as possible to a familiar hospital in the suburbs of Minneapolis. I could not have meant it more.

Just as I took that position, however, I was filled with overwhelming guilt. How could I ever challenge young people to go to the ends of the earth and serve God with a selfless love if I knew in my heart of this moment when I replied with a dramatic "No" to God? Even if I didn't tell anyone, I knew my integrity would be ruined forever.

And so a civil war unfolded—my will versus God's will. You know what that's like. In moments like those it seems as if life stops and everything we ever knew about God and ourselves is being weighed in the balances. A wrong decision then could alter the entire direction of one's life forever. A right decision could establish character qualities that could provide a template with which to measure countless future choices.

How long did it rage? It seemed like forever, but it was probably about an hour. I knew the only solution I could ever live with would be to give up—again. Yet one more time, I let Jesus be the Lord of all my life, including my future. At moments like that, we win when we give up. And, only as I gave up, did joy return to my soul.

In the margin of my Bible next to this passage in Luke 14, I wrote "August 1979." I like to benchmark moments like that in my Bible to help me never forget. I have other dates by that text. Each one represents a time when I asked at a significant moment in my life, *What does it mean to follow Jesus?*

The irony is that they never did find a kidney stone. Even when I came home on a flight classified as a medical emergency and I was given a kidney dye test in our local hospital, nothing was found. I passed the stone at some point without even being aware of it. While the doctors were screening me for a kidney stone, God was screening the quality of my devotion to him. All of them came up with nothing. Nothing, that is, until I surrendered my whole life to him again.

Years later I learned this prayer of Anselm which essentially I had prayed even then, "God's will: Nothing more! Nothing less! Nothing else! Amen!"

There is a cost to following Jesus. He wants us to be willing to take up our cross—whatever that might be for each of us.

WE MUST GIVE OUR ALL

Luke 14:33, "In the same way, those of you who do not give up everything you have cannot be my disciples."

The call to follow Jesus includes our love, our cross, and just in case there is anything left, we are called to give our all. Did Jesus really mean that? Is this to be taken literally? For some, God does ask this. The disciples left all and followed Jesus. Paul spoke of suffering the loss of all things (Phil. 3:7). Then there was the one young man's supreme sin because he refused to sell all and follow Jesus (Mark 10:21–22).

But I don't think he is calling all of us to literally do that. We can hold too tightly to that which God entrusts to us. We can get extremely possessive of our things and ignore that we are mere stewards and that he is the owner. The reality is that he is Lord of all or he is not Lord at all.

Our pronouns often deceive us. We can speak of our church and our house and our ministry and our future and our stuff.

I love the words a friend shared in our UVF chapel when he said, "Keep your fingerprints off the ark." Remember the story in the Old Testament about Uzzah who touched the ark of the covenant and instantly died (2 Sam. 6:7; 1 Chron. 13:10).

My friend went on to say, "If we touch the ark, it brings death, not life." I often think that our board of trustees or our faculty or alumni do not have a fingerprinting kit to dust UVF to see if my fingerprints are on it. But God knows. And he knows if I place my fingerprints on the UVF ark, then that will always bring death, not life.

The older I get, the easier it is to hold on to that which is most precious to me. Yet, if we are to follow Jesus, we are called to turn it all over to him. And we are called to do it over and over and over. In the words of Abraham Kuyper, "The Lord Jesus puts his finger on every inch of my existence and says, 'Mine! Mine! Mine!'"

William Borden and Frank Sinatra lived very different lives. Borden was born into the lap of luxury as an heir to the Borden Dairy estate.[3] For his high school graduation present in 1904, his parents gave the sixteen-year-old young man a trip around the world. He traveled through Asia, the Middle East, and Europe. The more places he visited, the more burdened he became for the hurting people of the world.

Finally, Borden wrote home about his desire to be a missionary. One friend expressed disbelief because he was "throwing himself away as a missionary." In response, Borden wrote two words in the back of his Bible: "No reserves."

In 1905 Borden arrived at Yale University where he was immediately seen as a person with a resolute mission to make a difference. During his Yale years, he focused on the needs of the Arabic-speaking Kansu people in China. Upon graduation from Yale, he turned down numerous high-paying job offers and in his Bible he wrote two more words: "No retreats."

He attended Princeton Seminary and after he graduated, he sailed for China, stopping over to learn Arabic in Egypt. While in Egypt, he contracted spinal meningitis and within a month, the twenty-five-year-old Borden was dead. Prior to his death, he had written two more words in his Bible. Underneath the words "No reserves" and "No retreats," he had written, "No regrets."

Frank Sinatra was born on December 12, 1915, in Hoboken, New Jersey. He began singing for tips at age eight. He was a rowdy teenager and dropped out of high school. He learned music by ear and never did learn how to read music. His mother persuaded him to join a local singing group and several years later was discovered by Tommy Dorsey. Over the years he reached the heights few musicians have ever reached with his influence, earning for him the Presidential Medal of Freedom awarded by President Ronald Reagan.

But one of the more significant contributions of his life was the way he popularized the Paul Anka song "My Way." The lyrics of "My Way" tell the story of a man who, near death, is comfortable how he dealt with all of the twists of his life while maintaining a certain degree of justification for how he had lived.

Since I knew some of the words and liked the tune, I guess I essentially consented to the primary idea behind the song, often belting out in a quasi-precocious style my own version of "I did it my way." But as I looked more closely at the words of the song, I discovered that the actual message of "My Way" is anything but funny. It speaks of a life lived for self with hardly any meaning beyond what it means to someone who did it "my way."

Robert Borden and Frank Sinatra were two very different men. One lived a short life devoted to following Jesus. The other lived a long life, doing it "my way."

Jim Elliot's words still challenge me and stir me to my core: "He is no fool who gives what he cannot keep to gain what he cannot lose."

Only as we keep following Jesus do we come to discover the true cost of following him. Oh, that we might say with Robert Borden at the end of our lives, "No reserves. No retreats. No regrets."

Allan Nelson has written a challenging book titled *Broken in the Right Place: How God Tames the Soul.* His opening illustration describes the process a wild stallion goes through under the watchful care of an experienced cowboy. He says,

> *Today was the beginning of the end of the stallion's self-centered life. His unbridled neck would soon be bound by the tightness of leather. His belly would constrict as the flinch fastened to hold the saddle in place. He would taste a metal bit for the first time. Today would mark a noticeable change in the animal's behavior.*[4]

According to Nelson, taming the soul is like that.
C. S. Lewis spoke of the same thing when he said,

> *Imagine yourself as a living house. God comes in to rebuild that house…But presently he starts knocking the house about in a way that hurts abominably and*

does not seem to make sense. What on earth is He up to?... You thought you were going to be made into a decent little cottage: but He is building a palace. He intends to come and live in it Himself.[5]

FOLLOWING THE LEADER

Every Christian leader must ask again and again, **What does it mean to be a follower of Jesus?** This question must be answered for our personal lives, but we must also answer it in view of our leadership responsibilities. Elton Trueblood must have had that in mind when he said, "We lead more by who we are than by what we do or say." Years ago I wrote this short poem which highlights the priority of being who God wants us to be over doing what God wants us to do.

> *Being is better than doing*
> *Because*
> *You can do and not be*
> *But*
> *You cannot be and not do.*

As leaders who are followers of Jesus, we must frame all our responsibilities by that relationship. In Christian colleges and universities, we often speak of integrating our faith with learning. In other words, every academic discipline from science to history and from psychology to literature and all others must integrate a Christian worldview into the content. A distinctive of Christian college or university education is that followers of Jesus apply what that means to their academic disciplines.

This integration means more than simply quoting a verse or two from the Bible to illustrate that academic discipline. It means more than using an example from sociology or mathematics or psychology to illustrate some biblical truth.

It does mean that scholars who are Jesus followers are thinking "Christianly" about every topic they teach. Because they follow Jesus, that commitment percolates through every academic subject so that it reflects a Christian worldview.

However, this integration is not merely something that scholars must do in a classroom. Christian leaders must also carry out this comprehensive integration as part of the administrative enterprise. Unfortunately, we don't hear as much about the integration of faith and administration as we do about the integration of faith and learning. But evidence of being a follower of Jesus must be found in the boardroom as well as in the classroom.

The second part of this book will address eight areas of administrative leadership that will be profoundly affected by leaders who are followers of Jesus. These Life Questions apply the Lofty Question, *What does it mean to be a follower of Jesus?* into the practical challenges which are a part of every Christian leader's responsibility.

For example, as a Jesus follower, what does that mean for how we write an organizational mission statement or design a strategic plan or even put a budget together? Should not integrity in advertising, honesty in organizational promises, or even relationships to the community in which we are located reflect whether or not we are followers of Jesus?

Even the subject of what we mean by *excellence* can be quite challenging for a Jesus follower. Over the years I have rarely found anyone who is not committed to excellence, but I have found those who don't want to be accountable for it. As a Jesus follower, how do you handle that? It takes enormous wisdom to embrace the value of excellence, and it takes great grace as a leader to hold others as well as ourselves accountable for it.

I once heard my friend Zollie Smith speak of our environmental witness. He wisely observed that even the appearance of our facilities reflects how well we are following Jesus. Do we have weeds in our flowers or is there junk everywhere or do the walls need painting and the carpets need cleaning? Here at UVF we often say of our old buildings, "We may be old but we don't have to be dirty." As Elton Trueblood said, "Holy shoddy is still shoddy."

Leaders who are followers of Jesus must be willing to be different. In his insightful book *Prophetic Untimeliness*, Os Guinness asks, "How have we Christians become so irrelevant when we have tried so hard to be relevant?"[6] The leadership style of a follower of Jesus should be distinctive.

In the chapters that follow we will apply this Lofty Question to eight aspects of leadership, which we will call the Life Questions.

CONCLUSION

One of my favorite places in Pennsylvania is at The Point in downtown Pittsburgh. Silent steel mills and modern skyscrapers witness the merging of the Allegheny River (325 miles long) and the Monongahela River (128 miles long), which there become the Ohio River.

Once joined together, their identity changes. Never again are they separate. Never again are they known as the Allegheny River and the Monongahela River. As the Ohio River they find their way to a whole new destiny. This new river flows for 981 miles until it joins and becomes the mighty Mississippi River.

That integration is similar to the integration that occurs when a follower of Jesus allows that commitment to permeate every part of his or her life, including all leadership responsibilities. It changes everything forever. It is no longer two separate entities.

What does it mean to be a follower of Jesus? We must keep asking and asking that question. Our personal lives and our public responsibilities depend on it.

PART II

THE LIFE QUESTIONS

CHAPTER 2

WHAT IS THE CULTURE OF THE ORGANIZATION?

The thing I have learned at IBM is that culture is everything.
Louis V. Gerstner, former CEO of IBM

Customers will never love a company
until the employees love it first.
Simon Sinek

The only thing of real importance that leaders do is
to create and manage culture. If you do not manage
culture, it manages you, and you may not even be
aware of the extent to which this is happening.
Edgar Schein

E veryone should step into another culture at least once in life. Each time Evie and I have done it, we always return home as different people with a new appreciation for here as well as for there.

I still remember our visit to the Central American country of Honduras. As our plane left Miami for the two-hour flight, we crossed the Everglades National Park and moments later we were out over the beautiful Caribbean Sea. The dotted islands of the Keys were off to our right and to our left was the island of Cuba.

It seemed as if I had read just a few pages of my book and we were already descending into San Pedro Sula, Honduras. My eyes were mesmerized by the sights as the plane gently banked to line up with the runway: palm trees, banana plantations, green mountains, and colorful foliage were everywhere.

The drive from the airport to the village of El Castano let me know immediately that Honduras is a different place from Pennsylvania. I was in a world of modern machines and machetes, fast moving cars/trucks and carts drawn by horses, and fresh-fruit stands along the road and a new Pizza Hut.

Neither pictures nor journals can capture the entirety of a cross-cultural experience. As a Jordanian guide said years ago, "What you are experiencing is definitely non-transportable."

When we refer to culture, this is usually what we have in mind. We think of far-off places with exotic foods and strange languages and unusual ways of doing almost everything.

This chapter, however, is not about the culture of another country. Rather, it is about the culture of an organization. A generic definition of organizational culture is that set of values, the way of thinking and believing and working, that exists in that place. My friend Dr. H. Robert (Bob) Rhoden describes organizational culture as the things people do without being told.

With those definitions in mind, effective leaders must know the culture of the organization they are going to join. This was perhaps the most critical life question Evie and I asked when my name was placed in the search process for president at the University of Valley Forge. Prior to my interview with the search committee, they sent me various institutional manuals and documents to give me a better idea of the institutional culture and values. Since the college was founded in 1939 and had gone through many stages of development over the years, these resources were important, but you can only learn so much by reading through documents.

I also talked with people who knew about the University of Valley Forge. The university had gone through some challenging years and at one time almost closed. There was also the matter of the campus. In 1976 the college moved to the site of the former Valley Forge General Hospital, which had been closed three years before. By 1996 many of the buildings had deteriorated, causing much of the campus to resemble a war zone. Even though I had grown up about an hour from there, I had never visited the campus. I could only imagine what it looked like.

I always liked it when Dr. Herman Rhode, one of my mentors, used to say, "There is never harm in walking through a possible open door. It helps you to pray more intelligently." Evie and I knew we had to step inside the space and visit with the leaders to "help us pray more intelligently." At the heart of our visit was the question, *What is the culture of the university?*

We will never forget arriving on campus for the first time. It was late on Saturday evening in mid-October, 1996. The sun had already gone down and the moonlit night created a sacred moment. The sign at the entrance assured us we were at the right place. We parked the car, turned down the window and just sat there, taking it all in.

We will never forget that moment: the four rows of stately oak trees; the expanse of the lawn; the dormitory lights; the

brick walls and white ionic pillars of the administration building. The stillness spoke volumes.

The sacred space of the campus informs a university culture but it does not define it. For us, we would understand
that more when we met with the search committee of the
board of trustees. During our interview we were asked a host
of important questions. The most critical question we had,
however, was this: *Will the style and tone and direction of
our leadership fit the culture of the University of Valley Forge?*

If together we didn't get that right, serving as president
may work for a year or two but eventually the institutional
inertia to go one direction and our leadership to go another
would create enormous cognitive dissonance. Inevitably, a
steep price would be paid and everyone would lose.

As the search committee interview unfolded, however, both
Evie and I felt enormous confirmation that we all wanted the
same preferred future for the university. We sensed within
the board of trustees a deep desire to move the question from
What is the culture of the university? to *What can be the culture
of the university?* The possibilities that the board of trustees
wanted were the same ones we wanted.

And though they had many other questions to ask us, we
felt our hearts were beating similarly regarding the organizational culture.

THE FORGE WAY

Perhaps looking more closely at one organization's culture
will be helpful. If you were to ask, *What is the culture of the*

University of Valley Forge? the clearest answer would be found in The Forge Way. At UVF, The Forge Way has become the way we describe the heart of our institutional culture. The Forge Way includes the institutional mission, vision, values, and outcomes.

UVF Mission: To prepare individuals for a life of service and leadership in the church and in the world. If you were to spend much time on the University of Valley Forge campus, you would not be here very long before you'd hear someone reference the university mission statement. You would discover that everything we do is all about the mission. We share it with our new students and new employees and new board of trustee members. We review it again and again with current members of the UVF family. Everything we do is because the mission of UVF matters.

The UVF Board of Trustees carefully crafted this mission statement in 1997 to capture accurately and comprehensively the purpose of the institution. According to best practices within organizations, particularly colleges and universities, an institution's mission statement should be revisited and reviewed at least every ten years or so. And though this has been done by the UVF board, the mission statement remains the same today as when it was first crafted.

UVF Vision: The University of Valley Forge will become a leading provider of Christ-centered, Pentecostal higher education in the Northeast and beyond. The UVF vision provides guidance and inspiration as to what the university is focused on achieving in the next five or ten or more years. Anyone who understands that vision knows there is an aspirational component within it. The process of becoming something more tomorrow than it is today inspires everyone to keep growing. UVF is also committed to a biblically sound and spiritually vibrant culture that extends here in the Northeast and around the world.

When an organization's mission statement is revisited, its vision and values should be as well.

UVF Values: The University of Valley Forge is a values-led university. Values matter because they describe what the university believes in and how it will behave. These deeply held beliefs and principles frame every part of the university's culture. At UVF, there are six core values that capture the spirit with which we carry out the mission and vision.

1. **We Believe:** We believe that the fullest expression of our relationship with God is found in a vibrant, authentic, Spirit-filled commitment to Christ.
2. **We Integrate:** We integrate faith and learning to maximize our personal and spiritual contributions to our families, churches, vocations, and communities in a balanced and healthy way.
3. **We Share:** We accept the responsibility to share the good news of Jesus Christ, both here and around the world.
4. **We Embrace:** We embrace community as a central expression of God's plan to transform individuals into the image of His Son, Jesus Christ.
5. **We Care:** We care for each other by promoting positive relationships that affirm the dignity of, and respect for, all people.

6. **We Create and Excel:** We serve and lead with creativity and excellence because our love for God compels our highest effort in every endeavor to glorify Him.

UVF Outcomes: As an educational resource center, the University provides undergraduate, graduate and other programs that prepare individuals to grow intellectually, physically, spiritually, and socially (Luke 2:52). When we speak of preparation we reference Luke 2:52, "Jesus grew in wisdom (intellectually) and stature (physically), and in favor with God (spiritually) and man (socially)." Everything we do inside and outside the classroom flows through those four developmental strategies.

But institutional learning takes place well beyond the classroom. Peter Senge's seminal book *The Fifth Discipline: The Art and Practice of the Learning Organization* also describes what UVF tries to model. He speaks of the need for organizations to keep learning and growing if they are to survive today.[1]

At UVF, the quest to keep on improving is marked by the often repeated, "What is the best year we have ever had?" The responsive answer has appropriately become, "The next one." Rarely does an event happen on campus without a time to debrief on how to improve it the next time. It is embedded in the culture.

I love Alfred North Whitehead's declaration, "Moral progress is impossible apart from an habitual vision of greatness." To capture the ongoing quest toward excellence, I sometimes say that a great college or university is one that really wants to become one.

In addition to these formal elements of The Forge Way at UVF, there are also many other informal nuances that are a part of the UVF culture. For example, we often say we will fight for harmony. Lest you think UVF tolerates contention, our cultural quality is just the opposite. How easy it is to allow toxic attitudes to fester because no one wants to take the lead and address them. I'll never forget the time I asked my administrative assistant to request something from an employee and that person replied, "Well, Dr. Meyer doesn't always get what Dr. Meyer wants." Of course that could have just been brushed aside, but if an organization is going to fight for harmony, it must be addressed.

I immediately went to that person's office and asked him if I had done something to offend him. The person seemed surprised and when I quoted his words back to him, he sort of shrugged his shoulders and with a jolly tone simply said, "Oh, I meant nothing by that. I was just kidding." In response, I asked if I could share how his comment sounded to me. And, after he said it was all right, I shared my concern, "I was afraid that I had done something awful to offend you because that bordered on sarcasm." Again, he said he meant nothing by it.

The main point of the exchange: We don't talk to each other like that at UVF. It is not part of our culture. Bob Rhoden often says that we all carry two buckets, one of water and the other of gasoline. When we encounter a potentially divisive issue, each of us has the choice to add a spoonful of water or a spoonful of gasoline. As someone said, "You can sail a ship with half a crew but you cannot sail a ship with a divided crew."

We also speak of our desire to be good neighbors. If an organization is to function well in a community, we must do our part to be good neighbors. In the spring of each year, for one day, UVF cancels all classes and everyone participates in

Community Service Day. Under student leadership, the entire campus is divided into approximately twenty-five teams to carry out the "ministry of sweat" in our community.

The day begins in the Flower Chapel where I share a short devotional. As part of my comments, I always explain that we do this for two reasons: First, because it's the right thing to do as good neighbors; second, because we want to inculcate our students with this altruistic spirit so they take it with them all over the world when they graduate.

On many occasions our local Pennsylvania senator, Andy Dinnimann, gives a word of appreciation and exhortation. From there we go out into our neighborhood practicing what it means to be good neighbors. I travel from site to site with Chuck Benz, a local banker whose bank helps sponsor the day, and together we encourage and interact with each team. At the end of the day, everyone has a special dinner in the dining commons to celebrate.

Being good neighbors occurs, however, more than just on that day. From our annual Christmas at Valley Forge concerts to athletic activities and from sponsoring Relay for Life and my serving on the boards of the Chamber of Commerce and the Phoenixville Hospital, UVF is immersed in our neighborhood. I love what Pastor Scott Wilson said when he encouraged local churches (and it applies to colleges and universities) that we not only want to do things *for* our communities; we also want to do things *with* our communities.

Creativity is another one of UVF's cultural distinctives. If you were to have a tour of the UVF campus you'd notice some distinct architecture. As indicated earlier, from 1943–1973 the property was the site of the Valley Forge General Hospital for the military. Wounded soldiers from World War II, the

Korean War, and the Vietnam War were cared for here. At the high point, three thousand patients and two thousand caregivers were present.

When the university moved here in 1976, three years after the hospital closed, there was ample evidence of the brick military construction. You wouldn't call this *classical* colonial architecture but rather *military* colonial architecture. Over the years many buildings were torn down, but all remaining old buildings have gone through some form of improvement.

When the Storms Research Center was opened in 2000, however, a new form of architectural vocabulary was introduced. Instead of primarily brick materials, glass and steel and concrete formed the modern, award-winning architectural style. I often like to say that even our architecture reflects our core cultural value of creativity. More new buildings have been added in this same creative vocabulary.

On the walls of the Flower Chapel are flags from every place in the world our alumni serve. Presently we have fifty-four flags. There is always an empty flagpole above the sound booth. That empty flagpole stands as a perpetual sentinel, calling out to all who see it of the existence of more places in the world where UVF alumni are needed.

At various times of the year, I say to the students, "Perhaps out of this year's graduating class another country will be reached so we can have another flag, because the harvest is still too great and the laborers are still too few." I continue by saying, "We will then have flag numbers 55, 56, 57, ..." By then the students count with me. I have had students on graduation day whisper to me as I shake their hands, "I am going to bring you the next flag."

These flags capture the missions or cross-cultural commitment in the culture at UVF. At UVF, missions is not merely a major or an academic department. It is a university-wide commitment. It's part of the culture. I will never forget the young man who said to me after we began the Digital Media major, "I am going to be UVF's first Digital Media missionary."

These are just a few of the formal and informal elements of the culture of UVF. I could mention the carillon bells, which call our students to class and chapel each day. They provide a cultural sound that connects deeply with alumni when they return, reminding them of the days they lived in the middle of this life-changing environment. In *Les Miserables* Jean Valjean was running from his nemesis and he stepped inside a monastery to hide. Over the next days the sounds of the bells and the singing of the children and the routines of the day are described this way, "All of these things informed his soul."[2]

I love that description. That is what organizational culture does to us.

Within the first year of being at UVF, I asked Dr. Billy DeSanto, chair of the Music Department, if the university had an alma mater song. He vaguely remembered one being referenced from years before but he didn't think it was ever sung on the current campus.

After some research he came to my office and played a version of it on a cassette recorder, which lets you know how many years ago that was. Some weeks later our College Choir sang it for the first time with Rev. Robert Krempels, the person who wrote the music for it, playing the piano. Now the choir sings that song on all special occasions, which adds to the deep cultural connection across the generations of alumni.

Universities provide many such opportunities to enhance the deep cultural realities of organizational life. From the naming of buildings after prominent alumni to the planting of trees for each graduating class, the very space of the campus is made sacred because of the rich meaning that has been added to what takes place here.

For anyone to be an effective leader, the question, *What is the culture of the organization?* must not only be understood; it must also be embraced. When I speak of these things, my heart rate picks up because I find them exciting and enriching. And, even though I am not a graduate of UVF, each one of them also "informs my soul."

I will always remember the conversation I had with a new employee of a few weeks who let me know he perceived that part of his role at UVF was to change the culture. We all know that any culture can be enhanced and part of our leadership responsibility is to do so. We do need that also at UVF. But, unfortunately, he was claiming the need to do that before he even had a chance to understand what was behind the present culture. If he had been allowed to change the culture immediately upon his arrival, the results could have been enormously negative.

ORGANIZATIONAL CULTURES

Few organizations do customer service like Nordstrom. In *Built to Last* by Collins and Porras, we learn of a "cult-like culture" which is so committed that somewhere around 50 percent of new employees are gone after one year because they can't serve the customers with the kind of passion Nordstrom requires.[3]

As Nordstrom says, "If you're not willing to do whatever it takes to make a customer happy—to personally deliver a suit to his hotel room, get down on your knees to fit a shoe, force yourself to smile when a customer is a real jerk—then you just don't belong here, period. Nobody tells you to be a customer service hero; it's just sort of expected."

It takes tenacious consistency to maintain that kind of culture. Success at Nordstrom necessitates an understanding and commitment to the culture of that organization. And anyone not inclined to embrace it should never try to work there.

Walmart also has a culture all its own. Sam Walton was known for giving over one hundred thousand Walmart associates this pledge in the 1980s, "Now, I want you to raise your right hand—and remember we say at Walmart, that a promise we make is a promise we keep—and I want you to repeat after me: From this day forward, I solemnly promise and declare that every time a customer comes within ten feet of me, I will smile, look him in the eye, and greet him. So help me Sam."

Sure, that seems a little corny, but it was the way Sam Walton perpetuated the Walmart culture. I remember the accountant son of Dr. Jim Allen, who was not allowed to carry a sack lunch because of the unprofessional image of the firm's culture it would convey. Any successful organization must have its team members understand and embrace and become advocates for the culture that defines it. Anything which hinders that alignment must be corrected.

I worked as a dishwasher during one summer while I was in college, and during my senior year I drove a school bus. Those were part-time roles and my engagement with the organizations was somewhat limited. But just after college, Evie and I went to northwestern Pennsylvania to pastor a small church. Only eight people made up the congregation and the position was not salaried. As a result, I had to be bivocational. I was able to find a position in the Right-of-Way Department of the Pennsylvania Department of Transportation (PennDOT).

I learned quickly, however, that the culture of a government agency like PennDOT was very different from a restaurant or a bus company. The PennDOT real estate appraisers and the architects interacted very differently from one another. I learned that even within one organizational culture there can be micro-cultures, depending on the immediate supervisor I might have.

The only way I was able to survive in those employment contexts was by observing the culture of the organizations and making the necessary adaptations to each one.

I have also served at three academic institutions: Continental Theological Seminary in Brussels, Belgium; North Central University in Minneapolis, Minnesota; and the University of Valley Forge in Phoenixville, Pennsylvania. Even though those three organizations are educational institutions with many similarities, each one has a very different culture, requiring adaptable leadership agility to adjust to each one in a unique way. A bilingual European educational institution is very different from an urban upper-Midwestern educational institution, which is very different from a Northeastern educational institution located in a beautiful small-town countryside just thirty-five miles northwest of Philadelphia.

CONCLUSION

Let us return to the question of this chapter: **What is the culture of this organization?** No amount of high grades or an ultra-impressive résumé will pre-empt the need to be able to answer this question. Our leadership hinges on it.

Although it has been nearly thirty years since Mark H. McCormack wrote his classic book *What They Don't Teach You at the Harvard Business School,* I am still thinking about it. At first the title caught my eye. One must be quite bold to criticize a Harvard University education.

But from the moment I started reading the book, I realized McCormack was not criticizing Harvard University. Rather, he was writing about the limitations of learning only from the classroom. His whole point was that some things you just can't learn from books or even from formal curriculum in an educational institution.

To be successful in life and in leadership, certain life skills must be mastered. He speaks of being able to read people. He said, "I can tell more about how someone is likely to react in a business situation from one round of golf than I can from a hundred hours of meetings."[4]

McCormack wisely observed that the effective leader needs to observe aggressively to pick up the nuances of tone and personality and style of those we are trying to lead or influence. We need to talk less and listen more. We need to "take a second look at first impressions" because they are not always accurate. Some things you just can't learn in the classroom.

That's probably why Tim Elmore wrote an essay titled "Helping Students Transition from Backpack to Briefcase."[5]

These soft skills that can't be learned in the classroom often make or break our leadership effectiveness. And, if we are ignorant of institutional culture, we might find ourselves going against the grain of the organization we are trying to influence.

Some effective pastors have been asked to serve as college or university presidents. Fortunately, many times it has worked with great success. But, unfortunately, any pastor who tries to lead an educational institution like a church will rarely be effective. Faculty cannot be treated like staff members in a church, and the board of trustees cannot function like a church board. The cultures are extremely different.

I do remember hearing of one such example when a person with a pastoral background was asked to serve as the president of a college. "Fortunately," I was told, "one of the first things he did was to unite the faculty. Unfortunately, they were all united against him." Most of the problems were caused by the difficulty of reading the different cultural signals.

I remember hearing a pastor friend who was invited to serve a new congregation. He wanted to begin well by bringing to the church special guests who could assist him in moving the congregation forward to the next level. Everything he tried got him nowhere. He brought in special speakers but they were barely tolerated. He invited contemporary musicians to come for concerts and again, they could not connect with the people.

On a whim he decided to bring a country-gospel group to the congregation. From the very first song, he couldn't believe the response. In his words, "I realized immediately that this congregation was country to the core." He finally understood the culture of the church, which made all the difference in the years that followed.

What is the culture of your organization? Unless you understand and identify with it, it will be nearly impossible for you to be an effective leader there.

CHAPTER 3

WHAT IS EXPECTED OF ME?

One machine can do the work of fifty ordinary men. No machine can do the work of one extraordinary man.
Elbert Hubbard

When your work speaks for itself, don't interrupt.
Henry J. Kaiser

A man of words, and not of deeds, is like a garden full of weeds. Thinking well is wise; planning well, wiser; doing well, wisest and best of all.
Persian Proverb

I f you had asked Francis A. Johnson the question, *What is expected of me?* he probably would have given you a very unusual answer. It all began on that cold day in March when, at age forty-six, he decided to do something about the annoying bits of baler twine clogging his manure spreader. He had always been a compulsive collector of old tools, farm machinery, and just about anything that might be valuable someday. By his own admission, he was so busy collecting things he never had time to date. He was still single when he died in his mid-eighties.

On that late winter day he began tying those bits of baler twine together. He wrapped his lengthening string together into a huge ball of twine. By the time he finished, over thirty years later, it was 13 feet tall, 44 feet in circumference, and weighed 21,140 pounds. It was long enough to go from his front yard in Darwin, Minnesota, to the Gulf of Mexico.

He made it into the *Guinness World Book of Records*. Tourists still stop by to observe this odorous tribute to his frugality and eccentricity.

From time to time, Mr. Johnson pulled up his lawn chair just to look at the ball of twine and contemplate his accomplishment. Before he died he reflected, "I still like to look at it. It's the greatest thing I ever did." He lived over eighty years and the high-water mark of his entire life was a smelly ball of twine that could be gone in a moment with one match.

Every leader must ask early and often this important question: **What is expected of me?** If we don't get this question right, we might find ourselves one day sitting on a lawn chair viewing our handiwork and concluding that the greatest thing we ever did was to build a big ball of twine. Bill Pierce said it this way, "For years and years I climbed the ladder rung by rung only to find out when I finally reached the top it was leaning against the wrong wall."

In this chapter we'll consider the details of the portfolio we are to carry out as leaders. This is usually captured in the organizational job description, which should help us understand the responsibilities we were hired to fulfill.

But for the Christian leader, our responsibilities go far beyond even the organizational job description. We must fulfill that job description within the ultimate context of what God expects of us. This ultimate obligation we will address later in Part III, Chapter 10.

THE JOB DESCRIPTION

On the first day Susan Resneck Pierce became president of the University of Puget Sound, she just walked around the hundred–acre campus. It was a beautiful day in July and there were not many people who were on campus at that time of the year. As she pondered the enormous responsibility that was upon her, she likened it to being a mother to her daughter, Sasha. Her daughter's welfare became all-consuming, and she anticipated that the same would occur with her role as president.

Pierce describes in the preface to her book *On Being Presidential* an encounter she had about a week later with her hair stylist. During their exchange the stylist asked Pierce what she did and she told her she was the president of the University of Puget Sound. Immediately the stylist asked her what presidents do.

Pierce tried to summarize as best she could and when she finished, the stylist paused a long time and then asked, "How did you get stuck with that job?"[1]

Over the years I have served in a variety of leadership roles and in each one I have asked the general question again and again, *What is expected of me?* I always particularized that question, however, with the specific portfolio I had at that time.

As I mentioned earlier, my first full-time leadership responsibility was to be the lead pastor of a small Assemblies of God church in Franklin, Pennsylvania. I was twenty-two years old and Evie and I had been married for less than one year. Although the church had been in existence for decades, there were only eight people who regularly attended. For the next seven years the question that dominated my leadership life was, *What does it mean to be the pastor of this congregation?*

That question became a part of my teaching and preaching ministry. Within the first few months, my college notes ran out. With no salary from the church (requiring me to be bivocational), how would I be able to prepare nutritious messages to feed the congregation? After much prayer and contemplation, God led me to lead the congregation in reading through the entire Bible by going through one book per week. We called it *Operation: Men and Women of the Book.*

As I read through the book a week before everyone else, I prepared a Bible study for Wednesday night and one of my Sunday messages from that book. Week after week I read and prepared. It took us two years. Later we did it again and I prepared new messages for my sermon on Sunday. I still have those Bible studies and sermon notes.

The question *What does it mean for me to be the pastor of this congregation?* kept me from running after fads or even teaching and preaching other peoples' material. It compelled me to probe deeply into God's Word and forge my own preaching and teaching style.

The church building, in actuality a remodeled house, was located on a one-way street next to a bar. Even though Franklin's population was only about ten thousand people at that time, we obviously struggled with visibility in the community. Again, the question *What does it mean to be the pastor of this congregation?* had to be asked to see the potential of what God could do in that community.

Because the congregation grew to over one hundred people, God led us to purchase property on the main road into town and there, over the next years, a new church was built, helping us to relocate to a much more visible location.

I kept asking that question regarding my emerging community role. In time I developed more and more relationships in the community, compelling me to keep answering that question differently.

As I said above, I kept working at the church and also at PennDOT as a bivocational pastor. As the weeks and months moved on, I kept asking myself what it meant for me to serve the church and the community in that way. Rather than use that PennDOT platform to preach sermons to coworkers during the week, I chose to live out my faith by being salt and light. Since I grew up in a Christian home, I had never really been around people who were not followers of Jesus. What a thrill it was, however, when my supervisor renewed his spiritual commitment and later became a board member in our church. Many other PennDOT friends began coming to our church. We jokingly said we should change the name of our church to "Highway Assembly of God" because so many in our congregation worked at the highway department.

But again, the ongoing process of asking that question informed everything about my pastoral responsibilities during those years. As the church kept changing and I kept changing, I kept asking and asking for seven years, *What does it mean to be the pastor of this growing and changing congregation?*

Then, just when the church was ready to support us full-time, Evie and I began to sense that our ministry might be coming to a close. After all those years and all that hard work and with the new church built, we really struggled with the possibility of leaving then. But, after a few months, we clearly sensed our ministry there was over and God was leading us on. Even then, however, it was that question which informed the timing of our departure.

Following a year at the Wheaton College Graduate School where I earned my master's degree, God opened the door for me to join the faculty at North Central University as a thirty-year-old professor. With that transition, my job description question changed to, *What does it mean to be a professor at North Central University?*

How excited I was to be in a setting where my seven years of practical, pastoral experience and my further graduate study could be integrated into a university classroom. But, I also knew if I made my classes ridiculously easy or ridiculously hard, I would unnecessarily discourage my students.

For the next three years my question was, *What does it mean for me to be a professor?* Everything I read and everyone I observed and everything I tried to learn informed that new question. There were large introductory classes and small upper division classes along with all kinds of assignments and exams and quizzes. With this process I kept changing and all around me the institution was changing and growing, which required me to keep on asking and answering this question.

During my third year of teaching I was invited to speak at a youth retreat in Fairbanks, Alaska, where a former student was the youth pastor. When I travel I always take leadership books with me and once again I packed several for this trip. One of them was Hudson T. Armerding's book *Leadership*.[2]

I read it in its entirety. And, as I read it, I sensed God was planting in my heart a burden for administrative ministry and that our ministry was going to change.

When I returned I shared this impression with Evie, but neither of us shared it with anyone. Within the next few weeks E. M. Clark, president of North Central University, resigned and shortly thereafter Dr. Don Argue, dean of the college, was asked to serve as the president. When he asked me to consider serving as the academic dean, God had already prepared my heart to say yes. I was thirty-three years old.

With that transition, a new question was before me, *What does it mean to be the academic dean (and later the vice president of academic affairs) of North Central University?* Over the next eighteen years that question was in the forefront of my entire administrative ministry. From the relationships with accrediting associations to curricular development and from interviewing faculty and serving on the senior administrative team, every part of my role in the academic enterprise was informed by that question. I never would have applied to the University of Minnesota and spent seven years to earn my PhD without taking that question into prayerful consideration.

After sixteen years, Dr. Don Argue transitioned to become the president of the National Association of Evangelicals, and Dr. Gordon Anderson became the president of North Central University. Since I reported directly to the president, I had to once again ask, *What does it mean for me to be the vice president of academic affairs of North Central University?* Over the previous sixteen years I had asked that question again and again, but serving with a new president required a whole set of new answers to that old question.

During the fall of 1996 someone placed my name in the search process for the presidency of the University of Valley Forge. God confirmed to the board of trustees and also to Evie and me that he was leading us back to Pennsylvania for this ministry. Suddenly, a new question was before me: *What does it mean to be the president of the University of Valley Forge?*

Since January 1997, that question has framed every part of my leadership responsibility. As a fifty-one-year-old new college president, I was anxious to find the answers to that question. I had to find out for myself if the Wheaton College president was accurate when he said, "In your first year of a college presidency you run absolutely as fast as you can. Then, after that, you pick up speed."

Although I had observed many gifted college presidents and learned immeasurably from them, the question for me shifted so that now I was responsible. It's like arriving in a foreign country and having a host take you from one place to another versus being your own navigator, responsible for each directional maneuver. It's much easier being the passenger, just going along for the ride, or even being the back seat driver making suggestions on how to improve the trip. When *you* are behind the wheel, however, everything changes.

I heard a new college president say it another way. "Before I became president I shot the arrows. After I became the president, I became the target."

I wish I could adequately express how important this question has been to me over these years since January 1997. These years have been marked by enormous change. At one point

I described that change as a metamorphosis by affirming "UVF has come out of its cocoon and is becoming a beautiful butterfly." From the organizational infrastructure to the campus facilities and from the academic programs to accreditation, UVF has changed. Bob Rhoden once graciously said, "UVF has gone from being a viable option to being a preferred option."

But my purpose for mentioning that here is not to chronicle all of the stories that have taken place at UVF over these years. Someday I'll write about them in more detail because I love to tell the stories. My purpose here is to share with you my view on a ministry going through a transformational doorway, and how one question kept marking that journey: *What does it mean to be president at the University of Valley Forge?*

During my first summer, I had the privilege of attending the New Presidents Seminar at Harvard University with thirty-nine other college and university presidents who had served no more than one year. In workshops and roundtable discussions, I inhaled idea after idea to help answer this question. I still go back to some of that material after all these years.

Also, during that summer (and many times since), I met with one of my most influential mentors, Dr. Robert E. Cooley, a former professor from college, later the president of Gordon-Conwell Theological Seminary, and now the chancellor of Gordon-Conwell Theological Seminary. His wisdom has been priceless to help me answer that question.

Obviously, UVF has changed dramatically over these years. I have changed dramatically over these years. That kind of change has required me to keep asking over and over and over, *What does it mean to be president of the University of Valley Forge?*

Perhaps the most challenging part of my role as president is in the realm of fundraising. Even when I was considering the possibility of accepting the invitation to come to UVF, I knew this would become one of my most important responsibilities. And, after all these years, I still must confess that I don't claim in any way to be an expert.

There are a few perspectives that I hold deeply, however. I refuse to take on an artificial persona to achieve fundraising objectives. The style of some fundraisers I've seen over the years does not fit me. I cannot be David in Saul's armor. Although there is much to learn to be effective, I cannot become someone else to do it.

Also, I refuse to be under pressure over the finances. UVF is not my university. I am a steward and my responsibilities have been entrusted to me by God. He is the Lord of the Harvest and the Sovereign One in control of UVF. This is his university, not mine.

These are some of the conclusions I reached in my new role as president. I wanted to develop a theology of fundraising that was true to biblical principles and also true to my own values and leadership gifts. I felt this was one of my answers to the question, *What does it mean to be the president of the University of Valley Forge?*

One of the most significant lessons regarding those values took place when we were raising funds for our first classroom building. God had blessed us with many campus improvements including a new library, a new residence hall, the demolition of twenty-seven old buildings, and the remodeling of most of the rest of the old buildings on our campus. But we did not have a signature academic building for classes. A famed Harvard professor once said that all you need for a university is a great professor at the end of one log and a great student at the other end. But most of the time in Pennsylvania, a roof really helps.

In January 2005 we began a capital campaign to raise funds for an academic building. Over the next six months God blessed us with modest progress. As yet, there was no huge gift to move the project strategically forward. And then, around June, I received a phone call from the Cardone family in Philadelphia asking if we had any projects at UVF that they could help with. I was extremely surprised with this call since none of us had presented our academic project to anyone in the Cardone family.

I shared the opportunity of this project and a few months later we learned of a significant gift to help build a sizable portion of the building. At that point, I did not know why the Cardone family had made this contact with us. I soon learned what was behind the phone call.

In the summer of 1935 Michael Cardone Sr. attended the Maranatha Bible Institute, Green Lane, Pennsylvania. This school eventually merged with several other schools to become UVF. After his summer session he wrote a letter dated July 17, 1935, to the president's wife, Alice Reynolds Flower (Mother Flower). In that letter Mr. Cardone expressed his gratitude to Mother Flower for the enormous influence of that school on his life.

In January 2005 when we were beginning our capital campaign for an academic building, a granddaughter of the

Flower family named Kathryn Ringer in Springfield, Missouri, was going through a box of Flower family memorabilia, and in the box she found that letter. She would not have known who Michael Cardone was except, in God's providence, her brother, John Flower, was a prominent salesman in Cardone Industries. She immediately recognized the name of the company Michael Cardone Sr. had founded, which today has over six thousand employees.

Ringer shared the letter with her brother and the next time he was in the main office he showed it to Michael Cardone Jr., the son of the author. When he read the letter and realized the content of the message, this deeply moved the Philadelphia businessman and with tears streaming down his face he said, "Our whole family is indebted to that school for its investment in my father so many years ago." And at that time, he and his wife, Jacquie, decided to make a significant gift to UVF.

When I first spoke to Michael Cardone Jr., he told me this story and then concluded, "The seeds for this gift were planted seventy years ago." I was born in 1945, which meant that gift was "planted" ten years before I was even born. That reality still leaves me in awe.

As these years have unfolded, I've experienced over and over how God has been faithful to answer prayer when the circumstances seemed impossible. I love to place the date of these miracles in the margin of my Bible next to Hebrews 11, the faith chapter. There are many dates on that page.

I have gone again and again to the heart of the question, *What does it mean for me to be president?* and again and again I am reminded that all I can do is be natural and then allow God to be supernatural.

YOUR JOB DESCRIPTION

I share these insights to help you understand how significant this question has been for my leadership journey. From my own interaction with the question, *What is expected of me?* I have tried to illustrate the ways I have kept asking this question over the years.

To help you, I suggest the following principles for you to keep in mind when you contemplate *What is expected of me?*

Continually Review Your Organizational Job Description. One of the challenges of married life is that individuals change and forget to tell each other. The same can happen with our organizational job description. I often think of the job description like the tithe. The tithe is a minimal standard of what is expected of us as stewards. Just as the tithe is a yardstick to measure our relationship to God, so the job description is a yardstick to measure our understanding of what the organization expects of us. Surely our leadership extends well beyond the job description we were given when we were invited to serve in that role, but it must at least start there.

I understand this may seem elementary, but if our supervisor has a different expectation of what we are to do, it might be because we are each reading the job description differently.

Always Own the Responsibility for What Is Expected of You. It would be extremely inappropriate for me to call Rev. Carl Colletti, the chairman of the UVF Board of Trustees, to ask him what is expected of me as president. He expects me to ask that question and make sure I am answering it in the ways which will best help the institution.

I cannot overemphasize the necessity for each of us as leaders to own this responsibility. Sure, I want to make sure I'm meeting the expectations of the UVF Board of Trustees, but it's my responsibility to understand what that means and to lead in such a way that what I do exceeds their expectations. Our supervisors will often coach us, but rarely should they ever have to hold our hand.

I've observed many passive leaders who are always waiting to be told what to do or they're waiting for their supervisor to solve their problems. Years ago at another institution the music practice room was not as warm as it should have been. The teacher's solution was to have all of the students bring their cold instruments into my office and, on her behalf, ask me to solve the problem. I still remember thinking she never really owned her responsibility with that dilemma. She never even tried to think of a solution. Effective leaders embrace their responsibilities by exceeding the guidelines written out in their job descriptions.

Constantly Be Aware of the Ever-Changing Expectations of You as a Leader. Change is coming at us faster than ever before. Our organizations must be more agile and we must get more done with less. And, unless we adapt, we will get bulldozed by those who do.

I remember getting a desktop computer in the early 1990s, and a computer specialist walked in my office and said, "Ah, I see you are moving into the '80s." Most of us who are in our sixties know that if we have significant technology questions, our grandchildren can help us better than most of us can help ourselves. I learned that when at six years of age our grandson, Noah, said, "Let's go online, Poppy."

Robert E. Quinn says in *Deep Change: Discovering the Leader Within*, "Each of us has the potential to change the world. Because the price of change is so high, we seldom take on the challenge. Our fears blind us to the possibilities of excellence—and yet another formidable insight. This insight concerns the price of not making deep change. That price is the choice of slow death, a meaningless and frustrating experience enmeshed in fear, anger, and helplessness, while moving surely toward what is most feared."[3]

Just recently I moved from a paper calendar to an electronic one. It seemed strange at first but the more I use it, the more comfortable I'm becoming. Too often Mac Anderson and Tom Feltenstein's book *Change Is Good... You Go First* is my preferred approach.[4]

Almost all of my creative writing has been done with a pen in my hand. My shelves are lined with notebooks in which are filed my handwritten sermon and Bible study notes. But finally—some may say at long last—this book is taking shape on my laptop keyboard. And I must confess that it's coming together faster this way. It certainly helps the editing and rewriting process. Also, I don't have as much paper on the floor.

Repeatedly Ask This Question. I am not married to the same person I was when we were married in 1967. Sure, Evie has the same name, but both of us have changed many times over. What it means for me to be Evie's husband may be the same question, but the answer I give is definitely not the same one I gave when we were just starting out.

I often meet strangers who ask what I do and inevitably they ask me how long I have been doing it. When I tell them I started in January 1997, I get all kinds of responses. I have heard it said that the average tenure of a college or university president is around seven years, and if he or she is still standing after more than that, it's a good sign. But none of us just wants to survive as a leader; we want to thrive.

What is expected of me? We also need to keep asking this question because the people who expect it of us keep changing. The same people around us have changing expectations. Also, all kinds of new people keep coming into our lives: new students, parents, friends, neighbors, alumni, employees, politicians, business people, etc. The list is endless.

And though we can't please everyone, we must understand the expectations of those around us. At one level, we don't care what others think of us and at another level, our entire leadership effectiveness hinges on it.

As we keep asking this question and implementing the answer, we may at times receive comments that are less than complimentary. Like Dr. Richard Dobbins once said, "It would be nice if everyone liked you, but it's not necessary."

And we can respond to the critics many ways. We can respond with, "The definition of a critic is one who stands in front of a masterpiece and makes noises." That kind of arrogance is never helpful. A more appropriate response would be, "Always listen to your critics. They may be the only ones telling you what you need to hear."

CONCLUSION

What is expected of me? This powerful question can move us forward personally and professionally. But even this question must be examined. Since we cannot do everything, we can take the advice of William James: "The art of being wise is the art of knowing what to overlook."

When we think about what is expected of us, we should also think about what is *not* expected of us. We should also ponder what we should not feel obligated to do.

Most of us have heard of Norman Vincent Peal's *The Power of Positive Thinking*.[5] Since it was first published in 1952, this self-help classic has sold around twenty million copies in forty-two languages.

For more than half a century untold millions have been transformed by this book, including me. My maternal grandmother introduced me to Peale's writings in my teenage years, and the positive effects remain with me to this day.

Yes, there is power in positive thinking. There is also a power in negative thinking. No, I'm not referring to the dangers of being a negative thinker. I am instead referring to the positive effects of saying no. We must feel free to ask, *What is not expected of me?*

Winston Churchill used to quote Alexander the Great who said, "The Persians would always be slaves because they did not know how to pronounce the word 'no.'"

Yes, there are times we must learn to say no. Emphasizing the negative can be enormously positive. An example: *right* versus *wrong*. We all know that. We know the catastrophic consequences if we cross certain lines. One stupid decision can ruin an entire life.

Other examples are *good* versus *better* and *better* versus *best*. Some choices can get very complicated. Priorities matter. Expectations can complicate our lives, blurring the lines between organizational expectations and family expectations. In his popular *Good to Great*, Jim Collins says, "Good is the enemy of the great."[6] He goes on to say that we don't have great schools, great government, or even great people because we settle for having good schools, good government and good people.

I remember some years ago when I was deep in research for my PhD dissertation at the University of Minnesota, my schedule was full and running over. Frequently my sons would ask, "Dad, can we go play tennis?" I had my academic goal to finish in five years, necessitated by the vocational question, **What is expected of me?** I was also working full time. I was focused and immersed in the tasks at hand. To what should I say "No"?

To this day I do not regret taking seven years to complete my degree rather than to sacrifice my best years with Darin and Kevin. We played tennis!

The gardener says no to the wrong plants (weeds) and grows a horticultural masterpiece. The author says no to the wrong words and writes a literary masterpiece. The sculptor says no to the unnecessary stone and carves an artistic masterpiece. The builder says no to the meaningless project and constructs a useful masterpiece.

Even Norman Vincent Peale's wife said no to him. Peale was in his fifties when he wrote his famous book and had received nothing but a stack of rejection slips. Dejected, he threw the manuscript into a wastebasket, and forbade his wife to remove it. She took him literally, the next day presenting the manuscript inside the wastebasket to the publisher who ultimately published Peale's book. The rest is history.

What is expected of me? Deciding what to do and what not to do could be the most important decisions you will ever make as a leader.

CHAPTER 4

HOW DO I LEAD WITH VISION?

*Moral progress is impossible apart from
an habitual vision of greatness.*
Alfred North Whitehead

Leadership is the capacity to transform vision into reality.
Warren Bennis

We are the people we have been waiting for.
Ngina Lythcott

How can we ever forget the life and influence of Mother Teresa. In 1992 George W. Cornell wrote an article for the Associated Press titled, "At 81, Mother Teresa's Mission Remains Unchanged." It begins this way:

Under the glittering chandeliers, an elite throng in sequined gowns and white dinner jackets filled the ballroom, the podium brimming with regally robed cardinals and archbishops. Into that scene of magisterial affluence at the Marriott Marquis Hotel on Times Square, a tiny slightly stooped old woman from the haunts of the wretched was led to the dais.

As if proclaiming the approach of a reigning monarch or president, the presiding officer boomed out,

'Mother Teresa of Calcutta.' The elegant crowd rose to its feet in a tide of sustained, admiring applause.

Her first words reflected her heart as she described how she sheltered a dying derelict crawling with worms, "It took three hours to pick from his body all the worms." The man gratefully responded that he had lived like "an animal," but now could die "like an angel."[1]

Cornell describes how Mother Teresa "declined to stay for the lavish dinner that evening," insisting that "any dinner honorarium for her should go to feed the hungry."

No wonder people called her "The Saint of the Gutters." Although she was awarded the Templeton Prize for the Progress in Religion in 1972 as well as the Nobel Peace Prize in 1977, it was her simple, selfless and deep compassion for the poor that made her a modern-day hero. That mission—and vision—never left her. It was the compass that guided her. It was the burden that pressed upon her. It was the priority that drove her.

Which brings us to the topic of this chapter, **How do you lead with vision?** J. Oswald Sanders said, "Eyes that look are common; eyes that see are rare." But all kinds of problems can hamper our visionary capacity. Whether it's cataracts that cloud our seeing or we're near-sighted or far-sighted, just because we have eyes does not mean we are able to see. Even dazzling lights can blur our vision.

A great story in 2 Kings 6:8–18 describes the importance of vision. Elisha, the man of God, was joined by his servant. Early one morning the servant got up and went out, only to see the army of the Arameans with horses and chariots surrounding the city. He asked Elisha a great question, "Oh no, my lord! What shall we do?"

In reply, Elisha said, "Don't be afraid. Those who are with us are more than those who are with them." And Elisha prayed, "Open his eyes, LORD, so that he may see." Then the Lord opened the servant's eyes, and he looked and saw the hills full of horses and chariots of fire all around Elisha. And a great victory followed.

The servant asked a question we often ask as leaders, *What shall we do?* In times of seismic change and limited resources and technological advances, we can lose our direction and our capacity to, as Max DuPree says, "define reality." This is a question which can come at us from all directions.

Elisha's prayer is the antidote, "Open his eyes, LORD, so that he may see."

In this chapter we will look at the question *How do I lead with vision?* from three perspectives: The Need for Vision; The Source of Vision; The Cost of Vision.

THE NEED FOR VISION

It doesn't take experts to tell us our world is in great need of leaders with vision. Catastrophes with the weather, civil war, famine, religious fanaticism, social and political upheaval take over just about every news cycle. After the genocide in his country, one missionary said, "There are no more devils left in hell; they are all in Rwanda."

In 1865 the dominant agrarian economy had 50 percent of the workers employed in agriculture. By 1945 during the industrial economy, the number of agricultural workers declined to 4 percent and those employed in manufacturing had grown to 40 percent. By the time the information economy was really getting started in 1996, the agricultural workers had decreased to 2 percent and manufacturing to 5 percent. Since then, these years have been made up of the creative destruction of much of life as we know it.

Researchers inform us that such large social change as we are experiencing now is rather rare in human history. These demographic, economic, cultural, and global currents rarely converge at the same time. But when they do, social institutions like families and churches and colleges tend to get left behind.

Jane Bryant Quinn captured the spirit of the times when she said, "If you are not confused by what is going on today, you don't understand it."

With all of this happening, some long for the good old days. Nostalgia takes over. They want to go back to when life was simple like during the days of Norman Rockwell, covered wagons and the little white church in the dale. But looking for those "good old days" is about as futile as sitting up on December 25 and looking up your chimney for a man in a red suit to appear. It isn't going to happen.

Others would rather drift with the change. Whatever the fad, they are the first to jump on the bandwagon. For them, change becomes the permit to do whatever voice cries the loudest. And so they go this way today and that way tomorrow.

Still others choose to do nothing, as though that helps. Doing nothing is like being in a canoe on the Niagara River as it moves closer and closer to the edge of the falls. Doing nothing doesn't change the inevitable results. These persons clutch their clichés and worn out methodologies, resembling the attachment of some to steel wagon wheels and the telegraph.

Though killed in a duel on January 29, 1837, near a frozen stream on the outskirts of St. Petersburg, Alexander Pushkin, Russia's greatest poet, had written sixteen years earlier words which in his day sounded as ours. They also had a need for vision.

> *I have outlasted all desire,*
> *My dreams and I have grown apart,*
> *My grief alone is left entire*
> *The gleanings of an empty heart.*

Proverbs 29:18 (KJV) says, "Where there is no vision, the people perish."

Today we need vision more than ever. Otherwise, enormous energy and time and resources will be wasted.

But where does vision come from?

THE SOURCE OF VISION

To answer the question, *How do I lead with vision?* we need to define the word *vision*. The word *vision* in the Bible is translated from two Hebrew and two Greek words, and they are found sixty-five times in the Old Testament and fourteen times in the New Testament. Abraham, Samuel, Nathan, Isaiah, Obadiah, Nahum, Habakkuk, Micah, and Daniel, along with the oral prophets, are described as being persons with vision. Often the revelation of the will and purposes of God came in the form of visions.

Negatively, the Bible gives examples of vain visions, false visions, a lack of vision, and even those who disobeyed the vision that was given by God. The prophet is often called a *seer*, a person with a heightened capacity to see. "To see" is found over six hundred times in the Bible, with many of the occasions describing the enlightenment that comes from God.

George Barna captures the essence of a biblical vision when he says, "Vision for ministry is a reflection of what God wants accomplished through you to build His kingdom."

But where does vision come from? I would suggest that vision can come from at least three sources.

From God: The Divine Source. One of the most familiar examples of a divine vision is from Isaiah 6 where the prophet has a vision of God, himself, and his world. That vision launched Isaiah's prophetic ministry, causing some to call him "The Silver-Tongued Prophet." His prophetic vision caused him to take hearers further into the future and hold them there longer than any other Old Testament prophet.

In Acts 26:19, the apostle Paul declared to King Agrippa, "So then, King Agrippa, I was not disobedient to the vision from heaven." Hebrews 11:13 speaks of those who appropriated the promises of God by faith even though they saw them way off in the distance.

For a host of biblical leaders, their vision was clearly God-given. They heard from God and that message became the passion of their hearts. They changed the course of history by their visionary leadership.

Anyone who lived in the Phoenixville, Pennsylvania, community from 1943 to 1973 could tell story after story about the history of the Valley Forge General Hospital and the hundreds of thousands of soldiers treated there during that time period. When the hospital closed in 1973 and until the UVF acquired eighty-four acres of it in 1976, the buildings quickly deteriorated.

Even after moving on site, most of the more than 1.5 million square feet of building space was not needed. As the years moved along, these dilapidated old military buildings soon gave a whole new definition to the term *deferred maintenance*. By 1996, the campus looked in many places like a war zone or ghetto with trees and vines growing out of the collapsed roofs and broken windows of those old buildings. The leadership had even considered relocating again, but under President Wesley Smith's leadership and with his encouragement, the board of trustees decided to stay.

During my first week as president in January 1997, a 1955 alumnus, Don Storms, met with me and asked me this question, "How big are your dreams for this school?" I was new and unsure what to say so I simply replied, "How large can they be? They can be as great as anything God has in store."

Within one year, Don and Ruth Storms made a $3 million commitment to build our first new building on campus, a library. They clearly felt that God was leading them to take such a bold step of faith. At a time when no one with financial means or leadership influence was stepping up with vision and hope for the future, the Stormses felt led by God to be the ones to do it. That commitment created an enormous positive updraft that influences us to this day. If the Stormses had anything, they had a vision for the University of Valley Forge that was birthed by God.

What if you are a leader and you are in a season where you don't have a vision from God? I think of our precious students here at UVF when they are starting out on their leadership journey. They may not be sure about the place of vision in their lives. They may have many interests but none that has yet become the passion of their lives.

Perhaps you have been in a place of leadership for a long time and your vision has become faint or even jaded. The easiest thing would be to walk away.

To anyone who is in need of a fresh leadership vision from God, the prayer of Elisha on behalf of his servant is still our best prayer, "Open his eyes, LORD, so that he may see." Only God can provide a vision like Don and Ruth Storms had. Only God can enhance our capacity to see as he sees. Only God is the ultimate source of any vision, whether that is for our own lives or for the organization we serve.

From People: The Human Sources. In the early 1980s North Central University did not have a gymnasium. The athletic teams had to drive from Minneapolis to St. Paul to use a rented gymnasium for their home games. I will never forget the day in chapel when the president, Dr. Don Argue, took two bricks and gently hit them together as a visionary signal of the bricks to someday be used on the campus to build a home gymnasium. During that same service he bounced a basketball on the platform, letting us hear that sound. Again and again he bounced it—up and down, up and down, up and down—until the echoes soaked into our souls.

Many who were there on that day still recall the drama of the moment. As he bounced that ball again and again he said, "Can you hear them? Can you hear them? Can you hear the basketballs bouncing in that new gymnasium?" And though plans had not yet been drawn, somehow that visionary leader inspired all of us to have vision also.

Yes, there is a divine source for our leadership vision. We can pray that God opens our eyes. But we also can pray that God uses the people around us, the human sources, to ignite a vision in us. George Bernard Shaw's words continually inspire us, "Some see things as they are and ask why. Others see things as they should be and ask why not."

Count Leo Nikolayevich Tolstoy was a man of towering moral presence, a giant Russian novelist, perhaps the greatest of them all. In 1988 A. N. Wilson published a biography of this man who lived from August 28, 1828, to November 7, 1912.[2] The book began in 1967 in a college classroom when Wilson listened to Professor R. V. Sampson talking of Tolstoy, beginning with the Jewish proverb, "If God came to live on earth, people would smash his windows." Sampson went on to say that people have been smashing Tolstoy's windows ever since he wrote. He spoke of the novelist who became a prophet as though he were divine. Wilson never got over the lecture.

Any aspiring author would do well to get close to Tolstoy.

Robert Henri wrote in *The Art Spirit*, "Artists have been looking at Rembrandt's drawings for 300 years. Thousands and thousands of remarkable drawings have been made since, but we are not yet done looking at Rembrandts. There is a life stirring in them."[3]

Any aspiring painter or artist would do well to get close to Rembrandt.

He was born on December 16, 1770, in Bonn, Germany. Ludwig van Beethoven's life was difficult, yet he had a lifelong sense of responsibility to God. Inner life tragedies, like his own deafness, marked his life. Frank Gaebelein said, "Thank God for this man whose music speaks so eloquently of struggle with affliction, of joy and humor of life, of sorrow and consolation, and serenity that surmounts suffering."

Any aspiring musician would do well to get close to Beethoven.

He died in 1905 but what a legacy Hudson Taylor left behind: The China Inland Mission. His son and daughter-in-law tell his story in *Hudson Taylor's Spiritual Secret*. On sacrifice he said, "Cross-loving men are needed."[4] On victory he said, "God does not give us overcoming life; He gives us life as we overcome." On adversity he said, "All these difficulties are only platforms for the manifestation of His grace, power and love."

Any aspiring missionary (or any follower of Jesus) would do well to get close to Hudson Taylor.

The more we can connect with those whose vision is greater than ours, the more it will inspire us and plant in us new visionary perspectives. I once wrote an essay on "Ten Teachers Who Changed My Life." The first was Harry Walters, my third grade teacher. Mr. Walters taught me in a one-room schoolhouse where his influence and reputation were legendary. He drilled his students on the fundamentals of reading, writing, and arithmetic. As a little boy, I was awed by this man.

In high school my hero was Cecil Williams. His interest in my family and me went far beyond his role as my agriculture and wood-shop teacher. He showed great personal care to my brother and me when our father died while we were in high school. I can still see this unspectacular man in his brown shop apron hold topsoil in his hands as he described its qualities and uses.

My undergraduate college experience was uniquely shaped by all of my professors, but six of them made a profound impact on my life that continues to this day. They were Robert Cooley (on discipline); Stanley Horton (on loving the Old Testament); Larry Hurtado (on homiletics); Donald Johns (on hard work; analytical Bible study); Anthony Palma (on biblical hermeneutics); and Glen Reed (on spiritual fervency).

Those undergraduate years changed my entire life. Ever since 1968 I have drawn visionary water from the reservoir filled during those eight semesters.

My favorite teacher, the one who influenced me the most, was a seventy-year-old semi-retired professor at the Wheaton Graduate School named Merrill C. Tenney. His quiet, scholarly manner in and out of the classroom profoundly affected all of his students. His PhD from Harvard University enhanced his impeccable scholarship and warm humility.

As soon as I had finished my master's degree, I set up an appointment with him to try to express my appreciation for his influence on my life. By that time I had been invited to serve as a professor at North Central University. I wanted to let him know how indebted to him I really was.

I'll never forget that meeting. After some preliminary conversation I finally got to the purpose of our meeting. Because I was about to begin my own teaching ministry, I began, "Dr. Tenney, if I can be half the teacher you are I feel I will be effective in the classroom." Of course, with all of his experience and impeccable degrees he could have said, "You're right," and he would have definitely been accurate.

Instead, he humbly replied, "Don't be a second Tenney; be a first Meyer. Be the person God has called you to be." The fragrance of that moment remains with me to this day.

My last formal academic experience was at the University of Minnesota. There I met Peter Patton, a true Renaissance man. From him I learned that an educated person could be interested in everything.

Vision can come directly from God's revelation. Vision can also come from those whom we allow to influence us. That influence can come from their lectures or their books or through their lives. Vision can also come when we encounter the needs of those around us.

Human Need: The Need Source. When Jesus looked and saw the multitudes of people, he was "moved with compassion" (Matt. 9:36 KJV). Seeing the need deeply moved the heart of Jesus.

1 John 3:17 says, "If anyone has material possessions and sees a brother or sister in need but has no pity on them, how can the love of God be in that person?" There is something about stepping into the space where a need exists and having the reality of that need go right to our soul.

That's part of the reason I love walking into the UVF dining commons, going table to table with a soda in hand, interacting one on one with our precious students. I love to ask them about how they are doing and what their challenges are. I love administrative ministry and sense God's call to do it, but when I look into the faces of our students, I am reminded again and again that the purpose behind administrative ministry is to help our students become all God wants them to become. They are the reason behind all that we do. And their needs inspire me and renew my vision to serve at UVF. Without them, we might as well close up shop and go home.

Nehemiah returned to Jerusalem and, after staying there three days, he and some friends went out at night to examine the condition of the city. Without telling the officials of his intentions, he looked over the plight of the city and then said in Nehemiah 2:17, "You see the trouble we are in: Jerusalem lies in ruins, and its gates have been burned with fire. Come, let us rebuild the wall of Jerusalem, and we will no longer be in disgrace."

Nehemiah saw the need. He identified with the need. He challenged those around him and they replied in Nehemiah 2:18, "Let us start rebuilding." So they began this good work.

Genuine need seen by genuine leaders will create genuine vision to get involved and get the job done.

Robert Moffatt was a missionary to Africa and on a furlough to his home land of England. A young Scotsman named David Livingston slipped into a service to hear Moffatt tell about his beloved Africa. Livingston was studying to be a doctor but decided to give his life as a service to God. He wanted to go to China but the opium wars were on and he could not go.

During Moffatt's message he simply said, "There is a vast plain to the north where I have sometimes seen, in the morning sun, the smoke of a thousand villages where no missionary has ever been." That sentence and especially the words "the smoke of a thousand villages" ignited something in Livingston. He had a new vision. He volunteered to go to Africa.

Livingston's vision burned so deeply into his soul that when he died, he had his heart buried in Africa and the rest of his body was taken back to his homeland for burial.

David Wilkerson's life was changed when he saw a photograph in *Life* magazine in 1957 while pastoring a small Assemblies of God church in Phillipsburg, Pennsylvania. In that magazine was an article about several New York City teenagers charged with murder. He traveled to New York City and asserted his voice to help those teenagers. Moved with compassion, he was drawn to the city in February 1959 where he began a street ministry called Teen Challenge, which today has more than five hundred centers in over seventy-five countries of the world.

Wilkerson's best-known book, *The Cross and the Switchblade,* captures his early experiences as a young country preacher in New York City and has sold over 50 million copies in over thirty different languages.[5]

The needs of those young teenagers ignited a vision in Wilkerson that has inspired the vision of countless others. I remember hearing him speak in the early 1960s. His message was mesmerizing to my young farm-boy heart. His vision helped grow a vision in me for those who were in need.

God can give a vision directly. God can give a vision through people. God can give a vision when we encounter human need.

THE COST OF VISION

If any vision is to be realized, however, there must be a willingness to pay the price for that vision. The following list shows why the price often can be very high for a vision to become a reality.

Risk. Whenever you step forward with vision, you will take a risk: a risk of failure or risk of embarrassment or risk of the unknown. Very little credit is given for failed attempts. And most places give only one swing at the bat. The greater the vision, the greater the risk.

No one gets a gold medal for jumping over two-inch hurdles or molehills. Abraham went out not knowing where he was going. Jesus took a huge risk with the woman caught in adultery when he said, "Let any one of you who is without sin be the first to throw a stone at her." In Galatians 2 (KJV) it says Paul "withstood him to the face."

During my first year as the president of the University of Valley Forge, a critical business decision had to be made. The risk was high. I sought counsel from my colleagues. I sought counsel from the UVF Board of Trustees. I sought counsel from my friend Michael Cardone, a wise and seasoned Philadelphia businessman. I will never forget his words of caution using a baseball metaphor, "For the University of Valley Forge it is the bottom of the ninth inning. You are behind and you have two outs. You cannot afford to make a major wrong decision or you will bankrupt the school."

But just because there is risk doesn't mean we should avoid the challenge that visionary leadership requires. I love the story about an international chess competition held years ago when a man named Frank Marshall made what has been called the greatest move ever in chess. He was playing the Russian master and they matched skill for skill. Marshall found his queen under serious attack. He considered his options and, since the queen is the most important offensive player, everyone assumed he would pull back.

Instead, Marshall used all of his time and then did the unthinkable—he placed his queen in the most vulnerable place on the board. Everyone gasped and thought he had given up, including his opponent. But as they studied the board more closely, they all saw that no matter how the queen was taken, his opponent would inevitably lose. And the Russian conceded the game.

The title of the *Reader's Digest* article telling this story is "It's Time to Sacrifice the Queen."[6] In everyone's life there come those defining moments when we must place that which is most precious out there and take the risk, no matter what.

Time. Visions can consume the visionary. It takes longer to grow an oak tree than a pumpkin. Irwin C. Hansen, CEO of Porter Memorial Hospital in Denver, Colorado, said, "You don't need talent to succeed. All you need is a big pot of glue. You smear some on your chair and some on the seat of your pants and you sit down and you stick with every project until you've done the best you can do."

I mentioned earlier the dates I place in the margin of my Bible next to Hebrews 11. These dates remind me of the ways God has worked to fulfill the visions he has planted in my heart. Of course, I want a vision to unfold like a time-lapse video photograph, but God doesn't grow roses like that. Nor does he run by a Timex watch.

Not many months after arriving at UVF I read in my personal devotions Hebrews 11:30 (KJV), "By faith the walls of Jericho fell down." And, in ink, I placed the letters UVF above the word "Jericho" in my Bible. People were praying long before Evie and I came to UVF that the dilapidated old buildings from the military hospital would be removed. We joined them.

Three years went by, from 1997 until 2000, and each day as I walked by those old buildings I kept joining my prayers with so many others who had prayed before me, "Oh God, somehow send us the resources to tear down these old buildings." There were some who wondered if they would ever come down since they had been the albatross around the neck of the campus for years and years.

When God answered all those prayers for what we called The Jericho Project (to bring the walls down), and twenty-seven crumbling, ugly, dangerous old buildings came down at a cost of nearly $2 million, we all recognized that it was a miracle of God's provision. God miraculously and creatively provided the $2 million to take them down. Sometimes the vision from God takes time.

Flexibility. The loftier the vision, the greater the need to be flexible. How easy it is to have the leadership disease called hardening of the categories. And the older I'm getting, the more challenging it is to be flexible. T. J. Jones, the British educator, used to say regarding preaching, "If you haven't struck oil in 20 minutes, stop boring."

I remember reading about a faculty member who had been granted a prestigious opportunity for growth. It involved the privilege to go overseas on a sabbatical and to soak in all the new experiences of that adventure. He refused, however, because he lamented, "But what about my plants?"

If Plan A does not work, look for Plan B. What is Plan B? We may have no idea, but if we are not willing to be flexible we will never find it.

Excellence. Part of the cost of vision is the price of excellence. Bursts of excellence are costly. They jeopardize mediocrity. Mediocrity doesn't like excellence and it will do everything it can to destroy it. I am always haunted by the title of Frank Schaeffer's book *Addicted to Mediocrity.*[7]

Vision will require passion and if the leader has passion, those nearby cannot help but notice. Rick Warren said, "If you want to know the temperature of an organization, put a thermometer in the leader's mouth."

It was July 15, 1838, when Ralph Waldo Emerson addressed a class at the Harvard Divinity School. He began, "I once heard a man who sorely tempted me to go to church no more."[8] He went on to describe that man's sermon on a spectacularly beautiful winter New England day. While the world outside was bursting with beauty, his eyes returned to the man in the pulpit. The contrast of life and death were almost more than he could handle. I guess that's why Charles Swindoll said, "It is a sin to bore people with the gospel."

This price of excellence must be paid over and over again. As Elton Trueblood said, "The struggle for excellence in any field is unremitting because men have to fight to retain heights just as they fight to scale them. The price of excellence is unremitting toil, constant self-control, and a continual disdain of the shoddy."[9]

I once heard of a man who had ridden a bicycle with crooked handlebars so long that when someone straightened them, he fell off. We really can become addicted to mediocrity.

Focus. I'll never forget my one-hour conversation with Henry Rosovsky. For eleven years he had served as the dean of the College of Arts and Sciences at Harvard University. He told me that he had been invited to be the president of the University of Chicago as well as Yale University. But in pondering those opportunities he had concluded that you just can't do it all. He had learned early and often when to say no.

I've heard some people say that the will of God is to find a need and fill it. I never have fully understood that because there are needs everywhere and to meet them would require us to go from this one to that one and never really know which one should receive our deepest commitment.

Unfortunately, most of our training (at least mine) has been to say *yes*. Learning to say *no* is unusually challenging.

Energy. Your vision will naturally set certain things in motion. It will take a lot of energy to get it started. That's the price, too. It takes six times more energy to start a flywheel from a dead stop as it does to keep it going. But once it is going, there is a relentless demand to keep it going.

We have all seen them at the start of the marathons. Everyone lines up with huge optimism. Goals are high. I don't think many expect to quit before they cross the finish line. But reality soon sets in and the runners spread out on the race. Many quit along the way. In spite of weeks and months and maybe even years of training, for some the price of the race is just too high.

Exodus 40:33 says, "So Moses finished the work." He followed through and completed the project. He maintained momentum to the end.

Sacrifice. In *The Seeking Heart* Fénelon said, "Allow yourself one excess: to be excessively obedient."[10] Sooner or later, every visionary leader will be called upon to place all that is most precious upon the altar. This will involve dying to all that matters. It is what Elizabeth Elliot called "The Glad Surrender."[11]

George Mueller knew what this meant when he said, "There was a day when I died." And as he spoke he bent lower until he almost touched the floor. Continuing he added, "Died to George Mueller, his opinions, his preferences, his tastes and will; died to the world and its approval or censure; died to the approval or blame even of my brethren or friends and since then I have studied only to show myself approved unto God."

This kind of commitment can only grow out of an authentic heart filled with integrity. Only then will the vision God has planted in the heart of the leader become realized.

CONCLUSION

How do I lead with vision? When the leader understands the need for vision, the source of vision and the cost of vision, then limitless possibilities are ahead. This question must be asked over and over. But no matter how hard we try to lead with vision, we are dependent on God for his empowerment to enable us to do it.

One of the greatest sermons I ever heard on our need for divine empowerment was preached by my friend David Owen in the chapel at North Central University. Pastor Owen was a Welshman whose distinguished pastoral ministry inspired all who heard him. As a young pastor I remember being awed by his anointed eloquence when he preached at our ministers' gatherings.

His message at North Central University captured the essence of that great text in 2 Corinthians 4:7 where it says, "But we have this treasure in jars of clay to show that this all-surpassing power is from God and not from us." And though he entered heaven a number of years ago, I can still hear his concluding words, which reverberated through that old chapel, just before he quoted 2 Corinthians 4:7 one more time, after which he pounded the pulpit and immediately sat down:

And so he always does it.

He brings forth his most prolific harvests from the most miry soil.

He transports his most precious cargo in the most battered ships. Hallelujah!

He accomplishes his highest end through the lowliest means.

He marches shepherd boys against military giants and simple slings against glittering swords and he wins. Hallelujah! And he wins. Praise God!

He brings down big trees with little axes.

He opens big doors with little keys.

He places the treasure in earthen vessels that the excellency of the power may be of God and not of us.

CHAPTER 5

What Does It Mean to Follow/Lead and to Lead/Follow?

*Every leader is a follower. No one commands
an organization without restraints.*
Larry R. Donnithorne

*You can only be over (in leadership) if you
can be under (in followership).*
James Leake

Beware of the shepherd who has rhinestones on his staff.
Anonymous

I love the parable of the teacup. As the story goes, it all began when a couple walked into an exclusive china shop. As they perused the exquisite craftsmanship on display, a particular teacup caught their eye. They went to pick it up and as they tenderly held it in their hands, it began to speak and this is the story it told.

A long time ago I was out in a field with no meaning. There the rain and snow and heat and cold battered me with all of its fury. One day a huge man with big boots came walking near me and with a sharp shovel he dug me out of the ground. Until then my life was without purpose but at least I was familiar with my surroundings and, more or less, comfortable with the way things were.

So I cried at the top of my voice, "Stop! Stop! Stop doing this to me." And he simply replied with two words, "Not yet."

This huge man with big boots took me and placed me in a large tub of water and with an old stick he stirred me round and round and round. Large chucks of my ugly and useless material settled to the bottom of the tub while the best of me floated to the top. As he stirred me I felt I was going to drown so again I cried at the top of my voice, "Stop! Stop! Stop doing this to me." And he simply replied with the same two words, "Not yet."

Then that huge man took his big hands and took the best of what was left of me off the top of that water and he placed me on a round plate. Well, I thought it was a plate until it started going round and round, faster and faster. And that huge man with those big hands started pounding me and pounding me while I was going round and round. He started forming me into a mysterious shape. I was getting dizzy and I felt I was going to die so I cried again at the top of my voice, "Stop! Stop! Stop doing this to me." And he simply replied with the same two words, "Not yet."

I thought he had stopped when he placed me in a small box and closed the door. It was only then that I realized it was getting hot in there. The temperature kept rising until I felt I couldn't take it anymore. Since

vant, 'Do

can only be
authority has
an organization.
nly has influence
authority granted
whom that person is

to someone. All leader-
follow. If you can't follow,

is subject from two perspec-
subject of learning to follow
the followership of Joshua and
before he became the leader of
llowed Moses' leadership for forty
ars he learned profound lessons that
when he became the leader. There are
earned as we follow those who lead us.
ok at the importance of continuing to
No matter what leadership role we have, we
countable. Followership really is job number
some of the practical challenges which I have
as I've wrestled with what it has meant for me
ntable as a leader. I will also share how I resolved
with my friend Dr. Don Argue.

there was a window in the door and I could see that
huge man, I yelled at the top of my voice, "Stop! Stop!
Stop doing this to me." And though I couldn't hear him,
I could read his lips and I knew he was saying the same
two words, "Not yet."

Finally, that huge man took me out of the hot box,
and placed me on a table. Whatever he was doing, I
hoped he was finished. And just as I began to relax and
thought he was finished, he began painting me with all
kinds of colors. I began choking from the smell and I
felt I could never survive the odor so I cried out, "Stop!
Stop! Stop doing this to me!" And he simply replied with
the same two words, "Not yet."

Again, he placed me in that small, square box only
this time the temperature was twice as hot. While the
heat kept getting higher and higher, the glaze fastened
itself to me and I was sure there was just no way I
could ever survive that. Again, I yelled at the top of my
voice, trying to let the huge man on the other side of the
window know how I felt, "Stop! Stop! Stop doing this
to me!" And again I heard nothing but again I could
read his lips and I knew he was saying the same two
words, "Not yet."

After a period of time that seemed like an eternity,
he opened the door of the box and he placed me on a
table. What happened next took me completely by surprise. That huge man with those big hands, the master
potter, picked up a mirror and held it in front of me
and I couldn't believe my eyes. He had made me into
this exquisitely beautiful teacup you are holding.

I love that parable. Just like the teacup, the process of becoming an effective leader can be long, painful, confusing, uncomfortable, and hard. But God wants to make exquisite leaders and there are no short cuts to that process. No one goes from a muddy field to a shelf in an exclusive china shop in one easy step.

No one goes from being a new follower to an effec[tive] leader in one step. It's a process that never ends. Follow[ing] leading as well as leading and following is a lifetim[e]

The question of this chapter is, **What does [it mean to] follow/lead and to lead/follow?** How do you [balance your] responsibilities as a leader and the relati[onship] with those to whom you are accountable?

One of the greatest challenges on my leadershi[p journey] involved this issue. It took place during the years I wa[s serv]ing as vice president of academic affairs at North Centr[al] University with Dr. Don Argue as president. He and I were dear friends (and are to this day) but we did not always agree on everything.

An issue arose where he and I had a strong disagreement. Over a period of several weeks we had from time to time discussed the pros and cons. It was obvious we were looking at the matter from very different perspectives.

I'll never forget the day he was in my office and we were talking about this again. We both knew a solution had to be found. On that day, he gave me his final decision and ended with these words, "And on this decision, I am digging in my heels." He had never talked to me that way. It would be impossible to express how upset I was.

LEARNING TO FOLLOW *BEFORE* YOU ARE A LEADER

We all know that it's impossible to isolate the moment we begin leading. A brief visit to a children's playground reveals immediately those children who have the word "leader" written all over them. And whether it is those naturally gifted children or all of the rest, each of them has a capacity for leadership influence.

During the elementary and high school years and even in college, we often speak of student leaders. There are seasons like that when a student is leading, but the predominant role is still to be a student. We use terms like *internships* and *apprentices* and *understudies*. Full-time employment with its correlative leadership responsibility will come later. And even after one is employed full time, most new employees do more following than leading.

Only four responses are allowed by a West Point cadet: "Yes, Sir!" "No Excuse, Sir!" "No, Sir!" "Sir, I do not understand." The soldiers are learning how to follow before they are to lead.

It's within that context that we reference *Learning to Follow Before You Are a Leader*. During this season we may receive more from those around us than we contribute to our leadership responsibilities. Our learning curve is steep. Our skills and our character are growing. The educator, Robert Frost, prayed for those in this season, "Lord, help them to build foundations which are strong enough to handle that which is eventually to be placed upon them."

That's what was going on in Joshua's life before the book of Joshua chapter 1. When we think of Joshua, we usually think of him as a leader, not a follower. The book of Joshua provided the historical bridge to show how Israel, the nomads, became Israel, the settlers. The first half of the book (chapters 1–12) describes the three phases of the conquest of the Promised Land, i.e., the central campaign; the southern campaign; and the northern campaign. The second half (chapters 13–24) describes the division of the land with the renewal of the covenant in Joshua chapter 24.

Throughout the book of Joshua, we see Joshua, a Moses-like figure who, with God's help, moved Israel into a whole new national experience. Soon, judges and kings took their place on the stage of salvation history.

But the story of Joshua does not begin in the book of Joshua. That's where he began as Moses' successor, but he is first mentioned in Exodus 17:9 when he is Joshua, the follower. Over the next forty years Joshua followed Moses and, as an understudy, he learned lesson after lesson that would serve him well when he was leading the children of Israel to cross the Jordan River and take the Promised Land.

For Joshua and for us, leadership rises and falls on our ability to follow. Here are a few of the lessons he learned:

Small Battles Precede Big Ones: Fight Well Now. (Ex. 17:8–15) In Exodus 13:17 God led the children of Israel away from the Philistines "though that [the way toward the Philistines] was shorter." He said, "If they face war, they might change their minds and return to Egypt." Rather than fight a big battle with the Philistines, God allowed them to face a smaller battle with the Amalekites.

After God gave them victory, God to Moses, "Write this on a scroll as something to be remembered and make sure that Joshua hears it." Joshua learned that the battles could get more challenging in the future. How critical it was that he learned well from the small battles. Those lessons would build his faith for the big ones that inevitably would follow. We later see in the book of Joshua the fierce battles which were to come with the Hittites, Amorites, Canaanites, Perizzites, Hivites, etc.

David fought the lion and bear, which prepared him for Goliath. Joshua 1:5 says, "No one will be able to stand against you all the days of your life." No leader starts out like that.

Establish Your Relationship with God : Connect Well Now. (Ex. 24:1–18) As a follower of Moses, Joshua experienced firsthand what was necessary to establish his relationship with God. The glory of God settled on Mt. Sinai. For forty days and forty nights this consuming fire of the presence of God was right there. Nothing would ever be able to take that initial encounter with God away from Joshua.

In Exodus 24 Joshua is right there with his mentor, Moses, as they obeyed God by building the altar and offering the sacrifices. In view of this lesson, Joshua 1:5 had to mean something special for Joshua, "As I was with Moses, so I will be with you; I will never leave you nor forsake you." Indeed, God has no leadership grandchildren. We each stand on our own with God.

Maintain Your Relationship with God: Abide Well Now. (Ex. 33:7–11) According to Exodus 33:11, "The LORD would speak to Moses face to face as a man speaks with his friend.

Then Moses would return to the camp but his young aide Joshua son of Nun did not leave the tent." Moses' relationship with God was not episodic or sporadic. Joshua experienced firsthand the face-to-face, ongoing relationship Moses had with God.

Early in his life Joshua did not leave the tent. At the Tent of Meeting where the presence of God was revealed to Moses, Joshua soaked up all he could, just like his mentor.

Compromise Is Always Costly: Commit Well Now. (Ex. 32:1–35) One of the darkest seasons in Israel's history surrounded the story of the golden calf. While Moses went up on the mountain to meet with God, the people quickly became corrupt and persuaded Aaron to make a golden calf idol. On his way down, Joshua heard the noise of the people and said, "There is the sound of war in the camp" (Ex. 32:17). To their dismay, however, they encountered the horrible compromise of the people of God.

When three thousand people died because of the judgment of God, Joshua recognized how expensive compromise can be. For Moses, the public sin of the golden calf caused all Israel to suffer. I wonder if Joshua thought of that day when, under his leadership, Achan's private sin was made public, causing all Israel again to suffer (Josh. 7).

We Really Do Need Each Other: Share Well Now. (Num. 11:4–35) Sometimes the follower must be corrected by the leader. Moses and Joshua were told that Eldad and Medad began to prophecy. Numbers 11:28 says, "Joshua son of Nun, who had been Moses' aide since youth, spoke up and said, 'Moses, my lord, stop them!'"

Numbers 11:29 continues, "But Moses replied, 'Are you jealous for my sake? I wish that all the LORD's people were prophets and that the LORD would put his Spirit on them!'" In other words, don't stop them, Joshua, we need all the help we can get. I love what my friend James Davis, co-founder of the Billion Soul Network, says: "If we are going to reach a billion souls, we must work together without egos and without logos."

Joshua learned that God could use anyone. He doesn't always work within our little boxes. Leadership must sometimes be shared.

Common Sense Always Helps: Learn Well Now. (Num. 13–14) The qualities of faith and courage are certainly seen in the story of the twelve spies. Ten of the spies, all leaders, lacked these qualities; Joshua and Caleb had them. But we must also always remember why the spies were sent out in the first place. They were told to check the land (good or bad), the people (strong or weak), the towns (unwalled or fortified), and the soil (fertile or not).

They were sent out to learn practical information about the place they were about to conquer, especially Jericho. Later in Joshua 2 he sent out two spies to do exactly the same thing. Sometimes the difference between success and failure for the leader is right there in front of us in the form of common sense. No wonder the follower should learn well now from the leader.

Listen for the Voice of God: Hear Well Now. (Num. 27:12–23) As Moses was nearing the end of his life, he was told by God, "Take Joshua son of Nun, a man in whom is the spirit of leadership, and lay your hand on him. Have him stand before

Eleazar the priest and the entire assembly and commission him in their presence."

As Joshua was transitioning from follower to leader, his mentor helped validate God's call on his life. Later, when he was about to fight the enemy in Joshua 5:13–15, it was the commander of the army of the Lord who met him in a very similar way that God had met his mentor by a burning bush. Joshua knew the voice of God would carry him through all that was ahead. God had spoken to Moses and now God had spoken to Joshua.

Leadership rises and falls on our ability to follow. As it was for Joshua, so it will be for us.

There is something to be said for experience. As Mark Twain said, "I knew a man who grabbed a cat by the tail and learned forty percent more about cats than the man who didn't."

Joshua was a different person after those forty years were over. Sure, he still had lots to learn. That never stops. Sure, he was still going to be accountable. That never stops. But those years of intense followership had uniquely prepared him for what was ahead.

I get nervous when I observe a student who is overanxious to get on the platform. Quintilian, the great Roman teacher of Oratory/Rhetoric, said of certain of his scholars, "They would be no doubt excellent students, if they were not already convinced of their knowledge."

Alicia Britt Chole captures the essence of this principle in her book *Anonymous: Jesus' Hidden Years...and Yours*.[2] She speaks of the "iceberg equation" where 90 percent is submerged in the unseen. She says, "Because of their enormous mass, with that proportion, icebergs are virtually indestructible." She eloquently describes that Jesus' hidden years make up 90 percent of his life. His public ministry lasted only three years, or 10 percent of his life.

Her formula for icebergs and life is *10% visible + 90% unseen = an indestructible life.* "Hidden years are the surprising birthplace of true spiritual greatness," Chole says. "The strongest influences on the decisions Jesus made in the desert were the choices he had been making before the desert. Every choice we make is an investment in a future we cannot see."[3]

Learning to follow before you are a leader will help you build a good foundation. Continuing to follow as you lead will help you lead well on that foundation.

CONTINUING TO FOLLOW *WHILE* YOU ARE A LEADER

I return to the dilemma I had with my friend and mentor and leader, Dr. Don Argue. When he stood there in my office and said, "On this one, I am digging in my heels," I hardly knew what to do. I must admit that just thinking about that moment brings it all back. His strong position made me realize he had made his decision and there was no way of changing his mind. I had a decision before me as to how I should respond. As I said above, my initial response was to comply with him in as gracious a manner as I could. But inside, I was frustrated.

I knew I had to get off campus to clear my head and heart. I actually wanted to leave and never look back. I realize now what a huge overreaction that was, but it was the emotion I felt at the time. Evie was the director of financial aid at NCU. I called her, but since she was unable to cancel a meeting she was in and couldn't leave campus right then, I decided to drive to Minnehaha Park, about fifteen minutes away, and just sort out my heart before God.

As soon as I parked my car, I walked to the falls. Just listening to the water cascading down on the rocks soothed my soul. My mind shifted to my dilemma. And, as I had grown accustomed to doing, I asked myself some more leadership questions. The first question I asked was, *Did God lead Evie and me to North Central University?* I quickly acknowledged that the answer was a resounding *yes.* There was no question that God had opened the door for us. After those seven years of pastoring and additional academic work, I used to tell Dr. Argue that I would have joined the faculty at half the salary. He would laugh and say he could still arrange that.

I then asked, *Is God leading us from North Central University? Is this a signal that our ministry here is coming to an end?* I was extremely frustrated, but when it came right down to the heart of the matter, I had to answer those questions with a resounding *no.* There was enough humanity in me to want to leave, but there was far more wisdom regarding the call of God to stop me from acting upon that emotional impulse. No matter how I felt, there was no way Evie and I were going to leave unless we felt God was redirecting us somewhere else. Clearly, we did not feel that way.

There was one more important set of questions to ask: *Did God lead Dr. Argue to become the president of North Central University?* Of course, my answer was yes. I never doubted that, but even asking it solidified something deep in me that helped me sort this out.

I then asked, *Does he have the authority to make that decision?* Again, he was the president and I was the vice president of academic affairs. He had the authority and the final responsibility for that decision. I later heard of this sign that was on the door outside another college president's office: "The occupant of this office may not always be right but the occupant is, after all, the president."

With those pieces of reality in place, what was I to do? I still felt I was right. Actually, I still do. I never doubted that. But my heart ached as I tried to find resolution. While looking at the falls and searching my heart, I realized there was only one solution. That season of time seemed to go on forever but finally I knew what I had to do. I had to die to my perspective and accept his leadership decision. That was one of the hardest leadership/followership decisions I have ever made.

Just because I was a leader with people accountable to me did not eliminate my responsibility to also be a follower. I knew I could only be "over if I could be under." I also knew I had to carry out my followership with the right spirit. There would be no value in complying on the outside while, at the same time, allowing a bitter spirit to fester inside of me. Unless we comprehensively die to ourselves in those moments, we can retain toxicity in our spirit that can poison everything.

Over the years I have met people who are angry because they have never resolved how to follow after they have become leaders. One of my friends had gone through great pain with his leader and it eventually caused him to leave the organization. Evie and I would often stop by to visit him and his wife. I always knew when his negativity was coming back because he led with these words, "The thing of it is, Meyer..." and he would go off railing on those who had mistreated him years and years before. He never settled in his spirit what it meant for him to lead/follow.

Here are three questions to guide you through these issues.

What Are Your Assumptions? I would share three important insights regarding your assumptions to help so that you are always continuing to follow while you are leading. First, make sure your assumptions are accurate. I must always assume that there is more to the issue than I know. As a follower I may not have all of the information. If I knew everything my leader knew, I may see it the same way as my leader sees it. And that is where trust comes in.

Second, I must always assume my leader has a perspective that I don't. That perspective can be caused by many issues, because I am probably looking at the parade through a knothole, but my leader has the benefit of a helicopter view. To help me understand this, Dr. Argue once said with a bit of a twinkle in his eye, "If you sat in this chair you would understand." To which I replied with a bit of a twinkle in my eye, "Then get rid of that chair."

Over the years I learned much from him. He was more experienced than I was. Even during those times when I disagreed with him, I reminded myself that he had a perspective I didn't have.

From him, I learned to give attention to detail. Whether it was crooked blinds or the unpolished shoes of a faculty candidate, he always gave attention to details.

I learned about the priority of family. He was never too busy for Pat or Laurie, Lee, Jon, their spouses and grandchildren.

Their annual vacations to the "holy land" in Banff, Canada, were always priorities.

I learned to have spiritual sensitivity. Whether it was in a chapel service or budget meeting, he always wanted God's will first.

I learned the advantage of a sense of humor. We still laugh at his behavior during the board meeting we conducted in the hospital while he was still heavily medicated from his knee surgery a few days before. We also still laugh at the lunch we had with a mutual friend who asked him, "What was your greatest surprise as president of North Central University?" After thinking for a moment he replied, "Being asked to serve as president" to which I facetiously said, "No, that wasn't your greatest surprise, it was ours."

I learned the value of hard work. Few colleagues arrived earlier or stayed later than he did.

I learned about having vision and excellence.

With all of that rich experience, I knew he had more experience in higher education than I did, making his perspectives broader and deeper than mine.

Third, I also knew that, ultimately, my leader had the responsibility to live with the consequences of his decisions. That did not fall on my shoulders. And at no time was he ultimately accountable to me. There were times when his decision would be final and he was right, and there were other times when he was wrong. There were times when he decided to agree with me and we found out I was right, and there were other times when I was wrong. Did we keep score? Were we ever justified in saying, "I told you so"? No, because the only time you keep score is if you are on different teams. We were both trying to do what was best. There were just those times when we approached things differently.

What Is Your View of Authority? Some people have unresolved issues with authority. It may be caused by poor role models from childhood or perhaps a very painful experience with a teacher in school or a supervisor at work. More than once, when I have struggled with the authority figures in my life, I've searched my heart to discover what's really behind my resistance. What's going on when I am expected to stand up and I find myself wanting to sit down?

Some people have a problem with the word *required*. Anytime anyone puts that word in front of an expectation, they bristle. Usually there is more going on than the issue of the request.

That's why the quality of our submission to God, our ultimate authority, finds expression in how we respond to our earthly authorities whom God has placed over us. No one can go into the presence of God and come out proud. When we submit everything to him and his lordship, any submission after that should be easy.

Of course, that's easier to write than to live.

How Do You Deal with Loyalty? Early on my leadership journey I used to think there were only two kinds of loyalty, i.e., blind loyalty and disloyalty. Blind loyalty would be described as the kind of loyalty that requires you to give blind support, no matter how wrong it may be or how much you disagree with it. No organization should ever require blind loyalty.

The only other option I thought possible was disloyalty. This allows you to support the leader on the surface or in public but in private you can express your actual perspective to anyone you want, rather than to the leader. The disloyal person shares with others their opposition, but to the leader, they act fully supportive. No organization can afford to tolerate disloyalty.

The University of Aberdeen had a promotional advertisement that said, "Great minds don't think alike. They just work together." But how can you work together and be loyal to each other?

Unfortunately, those two loyalty options can sicken and weaken the healthiest organization. It was Dr. Gordon Fee who helped me understand that there is another loyalty option. He called it *critical loyalty*. According to Fee, the degree to which you demonstrate your loyal support is the degree to which you earn the right to be critical. Loyal support does not mean that you must agree with everything that's going on. But it does mean that a message of affirmation must be equal to or greater than the words of criticism—and the criticism is shared directly to the leader and not to others.

Here is a profound principle. It's like a relational bank account. Unless there are more deposits than withdrawals, we will go bankrupt. Each time we express our support or affirmation, we're making a deposit. Each time we express our criticism, we're making a withdrawal. For some, that's easier to understand in a marriage relationship than in the complex macro- and micro-relationships of an organization. But the same principle applies.

You only hear from some people when they are complaining or criticizing something. It's hard to take that kind of person seriously because of their pattern of negativity. I know of few people who want to be like Alexander, the metalworker in 2 Timothy 4:14 of whom Paul said, "[he] did me a great deal of harm" and of him Paul warned Timothy, "You too should be on your guard against him." As Herman Rhode once said, "There is no more harm that can come to the Kingdom of God than that which is caused by a few carnal saints." And that negativity can poison the most positive organization and cause great pain to a leader.

Evie and I have been married over forty-seven years. She has told me she loves me over and over again. I have told her I love her over and over again. If there is anything we know, it's that we love each other. As a result of those positive expressions, when she corrects me, I know it's because she is trying to help me and wants the best for me.

I remember the time I came in the door and started fussing about something that had happened that day. The incident seemed to consume my spirit. In the middle of my remarks, Evie said to me, "Do you hear yourself?" It was like a knife to my heart. She had earned the right to share those words because there was no doubt in me that she had my best interest in mind.

CONCLUSION

Edward Norton Lorenz (1917–1987) served as a weather forecaster in World War II with the U.S. Air Corps. Following his military service he earned two degrees in meteorology from MIT where he later taught.

In 1961 Lorenz was using a numerical computer model to rerun a weather prediction, when, as a shortcut on a number in sequence, he entered the decimal .506 instead of entering the full .506127 the computer would hold. The result was a totally different weather scenario.

At the core of his findings was the realization that small differences in the initial conditions of dynamic systems, such as the atmosphere, could trigger huge and unexpected results. In 1972 his work led to the formation of what became known as the *butterfly effect,* a term taken from a paper titled, "Predictability: Does the Flap of a Butterfly's Wings in Brazil Set Off a Tornado in Texas?"

Lorenz documented what we know intuitively. Even our smallest initiatives can have huge effects—eventually. The butterfly effect can be applied to our leadership and followership. It can work for good or ill. We can set in motion amazing influence by the slightest right decision.

Can we do anything about the weather? Probably not, for as someone said, "Whether the weather will be fine; whether the weather will be not; whether the weather will be cold; whether the weather will be hot; we'll weather the weather, whatever the weather, whether we like it or not."

But we can do something about our followership. Each time we make a tiny choice and we allow ourselves to be under by following today, we can set in motion our leadership influence by being over tomorrow.

> *Over and under*
> *Under and over*
> *Over and under*
> *Under and over*

That is the never-ending essence of followership/leadership and leadership/followership.

CHAPTER 6

How Do I Effectively Manage My Time?

Bennis' First Law of Academic Pseudodynamics:
Routine work drives out non-routine work and
smothers to death all creative planning, all fundamental
change in the university—or any institution.
Warren Bennis

Bennis' Second Law of Academic Pseudodynamics:
Make whatever plans you will, you may be sure the
unexpected or the trivial will disturb and disrupt them.
Warren Bennis

You can't cram on the farm.
Stephen Covey

For forty-seven years he operated a huge crane. Every day his morning alarm clock frustrated him. Every day he got up, dressed, ate breakfast, and drove to his job. Every day his crane lifted tons of materials, moving them from here to there. Every day it was the same routine, over and over and over.

He began counting the days until his retirement and finally his morning alarm clock went off for the very last time. On that day everything was the same except for one small thing. He decided to take his alarm clock along with him to work.

He arrived and went through the same routine tasks he had done for forty-seven years. As the hours went by, he knew he was doing this for the last time in his life. Just as his day was about to end and he had moved the last materials from here to there, he climbed out of the cab of his crane. With his alarm clock in his hands he placed it on the platform where for forty-seven years he had picked up countless tons of materials. He climbed back in the cab, lifted his crane high into the air one last time. With forty-seven years of frustration caused by listening to that alarm clock each morning, he lowered that eighty-ton crane and smashed his alarm clock.

What a great feeling he had as his retirement officially began. Finally that old alarm clock could bother him no more. But even for him, time did not stop. It never does. Nor would it be easier for him to manage his time. It would only be different. New demands would crowd his schedule. A set of new obligations would vie for his attention. How often I have heard retired people say how busy they are and how they continue to struggle with getting everything done they feel obligated to do.

Sooner or later, no matter where we are on the journey of life, we struggle with time management. We only have so much time. The busiest person in the world has no more or less time than we do. And we soon learn that we are all terminal. No one gets out of this life alive. In an absolute sense, we cannot save time or hoard it. All we can do is use it.

Our question in this chapter is, **How do I effectively manage my time?** To be an effective leader, we must become good stewards of time and the only way we can do that is to manage it effectively. More college and university students fail for MOT (Misuse of Time) than IQ. More leaders fail for MOT than IQ.

Every Christian leader should develop a biblical theology of time. We place great emphasis on what it means to be ready for eternity, and we should. But each of us is entrusted with this precious, finite gift of time, and what we do with it will profoundly affect eternity, for us as well as for others.

Rev. John J. Paproski lived 34,555 amazing days. And it was at his funeral that I realized again that funerals have a striking way of reordering our priorities.

For ninety-four years Rev. Paproski lived his life to the full. He earned the Bronze Star in World War II. He golfed his age when he was eighty-four. He had a kind heart. His capacity to affirm his friends was legendary. From "I am so very proud of you" to "That was your best sermon. Billy Graham couldn't have done better," he oozed with encouragement. He was a father, grandfather, and great-grandfather, and the loving husband to Mary Florence for sixty-six years.

He was also an incredible preacher. In recent years he went to the pulpit without a Bible because he quoted his biblical references from memory. He was a leader of leaders. And that is why at the University of Valley Forge one of the residence halls is named after him: Paproski Hall.

But Rev. Paproski did not just live long. Evan Esar's words would definitely describe him, "You can't do anything about the length of your life, but you can do something about its width and depth." And he did.

That kind of life does not happen accidentally. It requires that we approach our time management strategy with passionate motivation. You have to want to. It also requires many practical techniques. You have to learn how to. Finally, you will need consistent discipline. You have to be willing to pay the price to. These three elements will help shape your whole approach to your use of time. In this chapter we will focus on each of these elements to help answer the question, *How do I effectively manage my time?*

The Bible also gives us insight into this question. In Job 8:9 we learn, "Our days on earth are but a shadow." Every time I address my own time management strategies I ponder how quickly a shadow moves from sun up to sun down. Time doesn't stand still.

Psalms 103:15–16 informs us, "The life of mortals is like grass, they flourish like a flower of the field; the wind blows over it and it is gone, and its place remembers it no more." This picture of time has always been vivid for me. As a former farmer and current weekend gardener, I have often seen the effect of the sun and wind on grass and flowers. Just outside our front door are huge hydrangeas that wilt the moment the temperature gets too hot. Day lilies last for a day and then they are gone. Time can be harsh.

I love the profound question of James 4:14, "What is your life? You are a mist that appears for a little while and then vanishes." There's a partial answer to that question within the verse when it says life is a mist, like a vapor, which appears and poof, it is gone. Time doesn't last forever.

The Bible also references two other practical items regarding time. In Psalms 90:10 we are reminded of the extent of time we have on earth when it says, "Our days may come to seventy years, or eighty, if our strength endures; yet the best of them are but trouble and sorrow, for they quickly pass and we fly away." Each of us has a divinely allotted amount of time on earth. It will not end one day early. It will not extend one day longer. We can't control the length of our time, but we can control the quality of our time.

To enhance the quality of our time, we must effectively manage it. This requires a deliberate strategy that musters all of our heart, mind, and will. Psalms 90:12 helps us frame that strategy, "Teach us to number our days, that we may gain a heart of wisdom." Effective time management will never happen unless we are extremely intentional. We must ask God for help to learn how to do it. We cannot do it on our own.

PASSIONATE MOTIVATION: WE HAVE TO WANT TO

Nothing great has ever been achieved without passionate motivation. You really have to want to. And effective time management is no exception. Deep inside we must have a white-hot fervency bursting with a deep desire to effectively manage our time. Lukewarm, casual consent will never work.

If you want to improve how you're currently managing your time, you will need to take inventory of how you are using it now. For example, if you are the kind of person who wants everything right now and you are not willing to defer that desire to a later time, your approach to time may need an adjustment. Brian Tracy understood this, "The ability to discipline yourself to delay gratification in the short term in order to enjoy greater rewards in the long term is the indispensable pre-requisite for success."

The famous marshmallow experiment captures this value. During the 1960s and the 1970s, Walter Mischel and his colleagues at Stanford University became fascinated by the strategies of preschool children to resist temptation. Their research was based on what four-year-olds did when given two options with a marshmallow.

They could either ring a bell at any point to call the experimenter and eat the marshmallow, or they could wait until the experimenter returned about fifteen minutes later and earn two marshmallows. The message was simple: receive a small reward now or a bigger reward later.

Some children immediately ate the marshmallow, while others delayed gratification and subsequently earned two marshmallows. The children who waited longer were re-evaluated as teenagers and adults and they revealed a significant array of advantages over their peers. Their social competence and self-confidence were much higher. As adults, they were less likely to have drug problems or other addictive behaviors, or to get divorced.

The marshmallow experiment is all about delayed gratification. Some children understood the value of delayed gratification; other children wanted to eat the marshmallow right away.

If you're the kind of person who resists delaying gratification for what you want right now, inevitably that will seep into your approach toward how you use your time. If you want to play first and work second, you will have ineffective time management.

How do I manage my time? I must be willing to delay gratification and deny the urge to say, "I want it now."

Some struggle with ineffective time management because they want everything to come easily. No effective time management effort will ever come easily. We will always have too much to do and too little time. It takes enormous energy to do it right. Nothing of worth comes easily, yet human nature cries out for the easy path. Lazy people will never manage their time effectively.

Branch Rickey was not a great baseball player, but he knew what it took to be a great baseball player. His greatest achievement took place on August 28, 1945, when he signed Jackie Robinson as the first black professional baseball player to break the color barrier. He also had a deep Christian faith, which motivated him throughout his career to never play or manage on a Sunday.

Rickey gave a speech where he said, "What is the greatest thing in the character of a great baseball player? I think it is the desire to be a great baseball player that dominates him; a desire so strong that it does not admit to anything that runs counter to it, a desire to excel that so confines him to a single purpose that nothing else matters."

Effective time management requires that same kind of desire. We really have to want to.

You also eventually must conclude that you can't do everything. We only have so much time. Somewhere along the way of developing effective time management, it will be necessary to decide what to do and what not to do. Although I first heard it years ago and have heard it repeated any number of times since, I still agree with the axiom, "The main thing is to keep the main thing the main thing."

I return to the words of Dr. Dean Hubbard, "There are a lot of things that need to be done in the world but you can't do them all." His encouragement helped to prepare a personal mission statement that enormously helped me to effectively focus my time. When I review it, I am helped with my choices of what to do and what not to do.

How do I effectively manage my time? We need a passionate commitment, which finds expression in the words, "We have to want to." Because at the end of our life, unless we have passionate motivation, there is no way we will be able to say these words, "Life isn't a journey to the grave with the intention of arriving safely in a well-preserved body, but rather to skid in sideways, chocolate in one hand, latte in the other, body thoroughly used up, totally worn out and screaming, 'Woohoo, WHAT A RIDE!'"

PRACTICAL TECHNIQUES:
WE HAVE TO LEARN HOW TO

Effective time management requires more than motivation. Without motivation, however, we will never engage ourselves in an overhaul of how we are using our time today. But, once we are motivated, motivation alone will not make us effective time managers. There are practical techniques that must be learned.

Never Forget How Valuable Time Is. When you have a lot of something, you don't think about the need to be a good steward of it. There was a time when getting an ice cream cone was a big deal for Evie and me. We were in our very first years of marriage and we were very poor. But we loved Dairy Queen ice cream. I can still remember cashing in Coke bottles so we could go to the Dairy Queen.

Evie loves hot fudge sundaes and she often craved them when she was pregnant. Because of our limited resources we struggled about whether we should order small or medium. I will also always remember driving home after having our summer refreshment and having to stop along the side of the road where the results of her nausea took its toll. We still laugh about that economic "loss."

Today we frequent Petrucci's, the delicious ice cream shop owned by John and Mary Colorusso. Today we don't cash in Coke bottles anymore. As we stand there talking to John and deciding what to order, I think less of what it will cost and more of what we want.

When I was young it seemed as though life would go on forever. Although my father's death during my high school years profoundly influenced my value of time, I still looked at this precious resource through immature eyes. Time was rarely on my mind.

My older brother, Ken, just turned seventy-one, and I am not too far behind. I value time more today than I did when I was in my 20s or 30s or 40s or 50s. When I look at the ages of our children, Darin and Kevin, as well our grandchild, Noah, I realize how valuable time really is.

If you are to be an effective time manager, you must always value time.

Look Carefully at Every Option for Your Use of Time. We have all said at one time or other that we don't have time for this or that. We try new things that seem important at the time, but we soon learn they really don't matter. Our garages and attics are often filled with evidence of incomplete projects that used up our precious time. I knew of one person who was going to make decorative pillows. He went at it with industrial-strength intentions but it soon fizzled, and the leftover materials stacked in his garage became a testimony to poorly used time.

To manage time effectively, we must be willing to look carefully at every time demand that comes at us. Some things are a matter of life or death, literally. We cannot defer them. If we don't take time to eat or sleep we will die. If we don't cultivate our private time with God we will die spiritually.

Even driving from Phoenixville to Pittsburgh will never happen if our gas tank is empty. I don't really have a choice. I must take time to stop and fill the tank.

When teaching on time management to university students, I have often encouraged them to analyze their time in fifteen-minute segments. Weigh it. Study it. Think about it. Get serious with it. If you think you have an unlimited supply, you will go about it casually. But you need to analyze it like an accountant analyzes a budget making every penny (second) count.

If you are to be an effective time manager, analyze carefully every option for the use of your time.

Just Say No: Some Things Just Don't Need to Be Done. Warren Buffet said, "The difference between successful people and very successful people is that very successful people say 'no' to almost everything."

Effective time managers know how to prune the demands on their time, just like gardeners prune their plants. We can get root-bound. Our centers can die. Old branches need to be removed so fresh life can emerge. Removing dead wood and deadheading are not optional. Too often we take on more obligations without eliminating others. Our lives get cluttered and we never have time to do what we really want and need to do.

How liberating it can be to apply this technique to our time management strategy. It reminds me of the advice given to a couple who always spent too much money when they went to the mall to go inside and yell at the top of their voices, "We don't need anything." Perhaps we need to do something like that with the demands on our time so we yell at the top of our voices, "I don't need to do everything."

I'm sure that's why Jim Collins suggested that we make a "Stop Doing" list to counter balance our "To Do" lists. We won't have time to say yes to the important things if we don't say no to the unimportant things.

Effective time managers learn how to just say no because there are some things that you just don't need to do.

Develop a Practical Time Management Plan. If you are ever going to effectively manage your time, eventually you're going to need a schedule. This will probably include a daily, weekly, monthly, and even yearly schedule. It may require you to get a calendar and lay it out on a table to see the big picture as well as the day-to-day picture.

I've done this since college. It has made a huge difference in how I approached my use of time. Some have told me, "I can't live by a time schedule because it will create bondage. I want freedom with my time."

To that person I ask, "Which would you rather have as your taskmaster, the demands which keep coming at you from all directions, creating enormous pressure or a time schedule which you set up based on the priorities you set for yourself?" There is nothing as fulfilling as knowing that you have planned your plan and you are working your plan. Otherwise, all of life is made up of giving attention to everyone else's priorities, and what really matters may never be done. Then the tyranny of the urgent will always win. The important just doesn't get done.

Here's a good place to prepare a kind of "bucket list" of all of the things you would eventually like to do. My dear niece, Beth Pears, did that during her twenty years of teaching high school literature. She gave her students the assignment to prepare a bucket list and she always showed hers as a model.

After a year-long battle with stomach cancer, at age forty-three she entered heaven. I'll never forget the hundreds and hundreds of her current and former students who came to her funeral and during their remarks, they mentioned that assignment. Before she died, she gave her mother a special request. "If any current or former student mentions the bucket list when they come by at my funeral to talk to you," she said, "please encourage them to add one more item to their bucket list—make sure you make it to heaven."

Beth had a sense of time that not only guided her in life but prepared her for eternity. She wanted others to have it too.

Effective time managers develop a practical time management plan.

Get Ready for Interruptions Because They Will Happen. Life is messy. It's filled with interruptions. We must be prepared for them. And, whatever you do, don't discard your time schedule because you have had one interruption. Even if you set up a time management plan for the month and you succeed with twenty out of thirty days or even fifteen out of thirty, you will still probably be much more efficient than if you had no plan at all.

I've often been challenged by the familiar saying, "I once complained to God because of all the interruptions to my ministry, only to realize *they* were my ministry."

Years ago I worked with a man named Art who lived about fifteen miles from the office where we served. I lived just a few blocks away. Although I was rarely late, I noticed that he always was there well in advance of my arrival. One day I asked him for his secret and he said, "Years ago my father taught me to always leave early enough so if I have flat a tire, I always have time to change it and still make it to work on time." His approach to time always anticipated the possibility of an interruption.

In a college or university setting I see students struggle with assignment deadlines. When I was a student I always tried to set my personal deadlines a week or two before the professors' deadlines. Then, if there was an interruption, it would come out of my schedule rather than my grade. It would also eliminate the need for me to make an excuse and ask for an exemption.

Even today I deeply dislike doing things at the last minute because there's always an interruption around the corner. Life is filled with interruptions. They are part of every project. We should not be surprised by them. And those interruptions can create enormous pressure. Some people say they do their best work under pressure. Others say they do their only work under pressure. Neither work well for me.

Effective time managers prepare for interruptions because they always happen.

Always Balance Your Time with Your Life Priorities. You will always regret the use of your time if it doesn't reflect a value system which is compatible with your Christian life. Don't use time for things that don't matter, causing you to lose that which matters most. Dedication is one thing, but no one should ruin health, marriage, or relationships with family because of an unbalanced use of time.

In Emory Griffin's book *The Mind Changers: The Art of Christian Persuasion,* one of his students who was a pastor's child asked him this haunting question, "Why do we always have to be last?"[1] Unfortunately, it isn't only the children of pastors who ask that question.

I'll never forget the pastor who confessed at a leadership seminar how he had scrambled the time priorities in his life. He described an incident that made him fully aware of his inability to manage his time effectively. The church where he served was experiencing phenomenal growth.

One afternoon his wife called him at the office informing him that his picture was on the cover of a prominent Christian magazine. He immediately ran out to his car and rushed home. He arrived in the driveway, parked his car, jumped out, slamming the door and as he ran inside he called out, "Where is it? I want to see it."

Just then his wife came around the corner holding up the magazine with the cover obvious for him to see. There on the cover was a candle burning on both ends. His wife was trying desperately to tell him something.

Effective time managers balance their time with their life priorities.

If Your Current Use of Time Is Not Working, Try Something New. Sometimes you have to attack time management as though you're looking for a cure for cancer. You may have tried all kinds of things and none of them have worked. That doesn't mean you should stop trying.

Have you ever heard someone say, "I'm sick and tired of being sick and tired"? If you're dissatisfied with the way you use your time, do something differently, anything. Over the years I have tested my sleeping habits to see if that would help how I manage my time. I do realize that I need more sleep as I'm getting older. But I will often experiment to try to improve my time management efficiency.

Evie and I regularly process creative approaches to our calendar. We both have our separate office calendars. We also have our personal calendar. We would never be able to manage all of the things we want to do or need to do without constantly refining our schedule and trying new ways to be more effective with time. We try this and if this doesn't work, we try that.

Effective time managers are always trying something new to improve their use of time.

Locate the Time of Your Peak Efficiency. An hour in the morning may be worth more than an hour in the evening. I find myself more creative at certain times of the day. I love mornings. I always have. Perhaps it was because I was raised on a farm and the early morning chores became a routine part of my life.

But there is no virtue in the morning. I have a friend who doesn't really begin to hit his sweet spot until midnight. That would never work for me, but then he doesn't prefer mornings the way I do, either.

Effective time managers locate the time of their peak efficiency and then leverage it to their greatest advantage.

Be Prepared to Do Whatever It Takes. Amy McNaughton is a runner. Every morning she gets up and runs. Years ago she made the decision to run no matter how she felt. In spite of the weather or anything else, she was prepared to do whatever it took to run. That decision informed how she uses her time, every day. Rather than fight a daily battle, she fought it once and for all at the beginning, and each day she just carries it out.

During the 2014 Winter Olympics I was amazed at the dedication of Meryl Davis and Charlie White when they took the figure skating gold medal. For seventeen years they prepared for that moment. They practiced as children. They practiced as they grew up. They were prepared to do whatever it took to win the gold for themselves and for the USA. What a moment that must have been for them when they stood on that podium with gold medals around their necks as they listened to their national anthem.

A young person said to a gifted opera star, "I would give anything if I could sing like that." To which she replied, "Would you be willing to give eight hours of practice a day for twelve years?"

Effective time managers are prepared to do whatever it takes to manage their time well.

Make Sure You Also Build Fun into Your Use of Time. Most of the time when people first hear of this kind of disciplined use of time, they assume life will be boring and filled with drudgery. For me, it's just the opposite. Never get in bondage to your time management plan. Build fun into your strategy. Life is not supposed to be one big work trip. Even Israel understood the principle of Sabbath. Time management must include work and play.

This is one of the primary reasons I've tried to maximize my early morning time. By getting things done early, I could more readily have ample time for Evie and our family. If it hasn't yet come through in my writing, I must admit I can have a tendency to be rather serious. Some of that is caused by my temperament, but I also desire to be a good steward of my time. Over the years Evie has been the true balance in my life. At times when I get task heavy, she helps hold me accountable so I don't go to far.

Her influence upon me began while we were in college. I met her during the spring semester of my sophomore year. We had already sensed God was doing something special in our lives. She went home to Zion, Illinois, for the summer and I went home to the farm just outside of Lebanon, Pennsylvania. We wrote and called often over the summer as our love continued to grow.

When we returned to college in the fall, I had a full schedule. Because I was a serious student and had numerous leadership responsibilities, within the first week I set up my time schedule for the year. What I am about to share with you is hard for me to admit, but since I started this story, I guess I must complete it.

On my schedule I had set the time for Evie and me to be together each day from 9:00 p.m. to 9:15 p.m. I actually allocated only fifteen minutes each day for "us." I still can't believe I did that, but I did.

The time came for me to share with her my wonderful plan for the year. Needless to say, she was not very happy with my "wonderful plan" and it took much longer than fifteen minutes for us to discuss this and for me to make the much-needed revisions. To this day I'm profoundly grateful that she had the grace and courage to help me build work and play and relationship into my time management plan. And she still does.

Effective time managers must make sure they build fun into their approach to time.

COMMITTED DISCIPLINE:
WE HAVE TO PAY THE PRICE TO

No amount of passionate motivation or practical techniques to help us effectively manage our time will ever make a difference if we do not have committed discipline to pay the price to make it happen. You have to be willing to pay the price to. And there is always a price.

John Milton said, "The flourishing and decaying of all civil societies, all moments and turnings of human occasions are moved to and fro upon the axle of discipline." It takes enormous discipline to effectively manage our time.

"Everything is a tradeoff." That's what the waitress said to Evie and me when we declined bread before dinner because we wanted to save room for dessert. In time management, everything is a tradeoff too.

We tell our students at UVF, "Groans today; gratitude tomorrow." If we pay the price of discipline with the way we manage time today by learning to speak that language now or play that instrument now or save that money now or cultivate that grace now, we will never look back with regret. But without committed discipline, it will likely never happen.

Committed discipline for effective time management means we must make sure we have developed a sound rationale for doing what we are doing. It must make sense. There is no room for high and lofty idealism. Our feet must be on the ground; our sleeves must be rolled up; and our will must be set in motion.

Committed discipline for effective time management requires that we be willing to accept boundaries in our lives. Boundaries are always necessary. If your motto is "I don't want to have to," managing your time well will probably never happen. If something is outside the realm of that which will help you to be effective with your time, let it go. For some, having an accountability person can also help.

Committed discipline for effective time management also includes the capacity to look beyond today. My friend Dick Foth began a sermon with the words, "If I could give you a gift today, it would be the gift of perspective." Our approach to time should always have the perspective of eternity on the horizon. Ultimately, we are responsible to God for our stewardship of time.

Committed discipline for effective time management can never succeed unless God provides the help. With our use of time (as well as all of life), "Without him we can do nothing."

CONCLUSION

How can I effectively manage my time? Psalms 90:12 says, "Teach us to number our days, that we may gain a heart of wisdom."

The stakes are huge because, as James Menzie said, "Life is a one-time opportunity."

William Shakespeare summed up the meaning of life like this:

> *Tomorrow and tomorrow and tomorrow*
> *Creeps in this petty pace from day to day*
> *To the last syllable of recorded time.*
> *And all our yesterdays have lighted fools*
> *The way to dusty death. Out, out brief candle.*
> *Life's but a walking shadow, a poor player*
> *That struts and frets his hour upon the stage,*
> *And then is heard no more. It is a tale*
> *Told by an idiot, full of sound and fury*
> *Signifying nothing.*

On the other hand, Bob Benson had a different view of time in his profound poem "Life Is So Daily."[2]

> *Nearly everything I do*
> *needs doing again so soon.*
> *Most everything I did today*
> *has to be redone tomorrow*

or at least
     by the end of the week:
shaving, eating,
          driving to work,
     cleaning the gutters,
          building a fire,
     answering the mail,
          keeping up with the Joneses,
          talking on the phone.

All these,
          and a hundred other things,
     make up my waking hours
          day after day,
          week after week,
until at times it seems that
          most of my life is spent
     in a succession of marches
          that do not matter
     and numberless causes
          that do not count.

And I am made to wonder:
          Will I give myself away
          bit by bit—
     time, thought,
          energy, love,
          emotion, will—
to a collection
     of choices and projects
which will die as I do,
          because they mattered only
          to me?

Somehow may I use
the lumber of my life
to build a ladder—
straight, sturdy, true—
on which people may climb
until they come to thee.
Or to fashion a cathedral—
a quiet, holy place
where people would pause
and seek thy ways.
Or to plant a tree—
tall, serene, fruitful—
whose shade would someday
grant a traveler rest.

Let me share
in thy works,
not asking that I must see
the results in my day,
but laboring
in this confidence:
Because it was done in thee,
it will someday
come to fulfillment
and I will not have lived
worthlessly, selfishly,
needlessly.

That will only happen if we effectively manage our time!

CHAPTER 7

HOW DO I BALANCE MY PUBLIC LIFE AND MY PRIVATE LIFE?

Truth is like a bird; it cannot fly on one wing. Yet we are forever trying to take off with one wing flapping furiously while the other is tucked neatly out of sight.
A. W. Tozer

No one can be a public person without risk to his soul, unless first he is a private person.
Thomas à Kempis

Self-care is never a selfish act.
Parker J. Palmer

BTK (Bind, Torture, Kill) will forever identify Dennis Rader. Those were the words he chose to describe a string of murders (at least ten) he committed in Wichita, Kansas, back to 1974. Though a Scout leader, husband, father, and town dogcatcher in a working-class suburb where he had lived more than thirty years, this man will be forever known for his heinous crimes.

"At Christ Lutheran Church," Patrick O'Driscoll said when he found out who he was, "Dennis Raider was known as a caring man, an usher who was president of the church council. He even brought salad and spaghetti sauce to a church supper he couldn't attend."

At the time of his arrest one writer asked this haunting question, "How could BTK have juggled two lives for more than three decades?" All of us should think about that question. I realize BTK is an ultimate extreme of leading a double life, but how is it possible to become such a person? How can a man function simultaneously in such good and bad worlds and seem on the outside to be normal?

Parker J. Palmer addresses this subject in his book *A Hidden Wholeness: The Journey Toward an Undivided Life.* His words are profound. "I pay a steep price when I live a divided life—feeling fraudulent, anxious about being found out, and depressed by the fact that I am denying my own selfhood. The people around me pay a price as well, for now they walk on ground made unstable by my dividedness."[1]

He continues, "A fault line runs down the middle of my life, and whenever it cracks open—divorcing my words and actions from the truth I hold within—things around me get shaky and start to fall apart."

How do I balance my public life and my private life? If we don't cultivate a healthy balance between the public life of our private person and the private life of our public person, our leadership is doomed to fail. Obviously, one small gesture without integrity does not make anyone like Dennis Rader. But even Dennis Rader did not become BTK overnight.

A. W. Tozer said, "Truth is like a bird; it cannot fly on one wing. Yet we are forever trying to take off with one wing flapping furiously while the other is tucked neatly out of sight."

The Bible references the public and private sides of David's life in Psalms 78:72, "David shepherded them with integrity of heart [character]; with skillful hands he led them [competence]." They are like the two sides of the same coin. You can't separate them. One is just external and visible; the other is internal and invisible.

The year was 1170 AD in the city of Pisa, Italy, when they began building the Cathedral Bell Tower. For 176 years they built it until it reached its height of 179 feet. The tower was only 35 feet high when they saw that, due to the unequal settling of the foundation, it had begun to lean.

Today it stands about 18 feet off perpendicular. Engineers considered several options to correct the problem. One of them suggested building a huge human figure with the silhouette of a person leaning up against the Bell Tower. Even though it may have helped, that idea didn't get much favor. They eventually designed and installed an intricate set of cables and weights to counter the force of gravity and that has actually helped. Without correction, however, the Leaning Tower of Pisa would inevitably collapse.

You can't see the foundation of that historic building, but you can't avoid seeing the results of its deficiency.

That is exactly why this subject matters so much. *How do you balance your public life and your private life?* That question requires vigilant attention for the leader. The tug of war between the two is relentless. Overemphasis on one or the other can render our leadership influence anemic.

One of the first things I do when a subject like this arises is to find out what the Bible says about it. I decided to read through the Bible looking for these public and private sides of the people of God. I was amazed at the frequent references to this topic. It seemed as if I could hardly turn a page without finding at least one reference.

One of the clearest examples is found in the life of Elijah. In 1 Kings 17:3–4 Elijah is told to "Leave here, turn eastward and hide in the Kerith Ravine, east of the Jordon. You will drink from the brook, and I have directed the ravens to supply you with food there." Go hide yourself is a clear description of a private season in Elijah's life. Special things took place in him during that season.

In 1 Kings 18:1 Elijah is told to "Go and present yourself to Ahab, and I will send rain on the land." Go and present yourself is a clear description of a public season in Elijah's life. Special things took place through him during that season.

For Elijah, there was a time to hide and a time to show. There was a season when he was private; there was a season when he was public. God worked uniquely during each of those seasons.

In the book of Numbers the Levites were chosen by God and were taken from all of the tribes for his special calling. The Levites were also given to all tribes for specific tasks around the tabernacle. They had clear job descriptions, including the task of setting the tabernacle up and taking it down. There was a private dimension to their calling and a public dimension to their calling. The private dimension related to their personal lives because God had chosen them as his special leaders out of all the other tribes of Israel. The public dimension related to their place of service to the rest of the children of Israel because God had given them unique service responsibilities.

Numerous references from the lives of Abraham, Moses, Samuel, David, Isaiah, Ezekiel, and many other Old Testament leaders show these two parts in each of their lives. The basic content of the Historical Books captures predominantly the public side of the people of God. It's like watching them act out human history on the public stage for all to see.

The basic content of the Poetic Books, however, captures predominantly the private side of the people of God. It's like going behind the stage into their dressing rooms and watching them in private in their personal devotions.

Jesus' life is our ultimate model of a life well lived in public as well as in private. Again and again "Jesus often withdrew to lonely places and prayed" (Luke 5:16). Whether he was led by the Spirit into the desert (Matt. 4:1) or he went into the hills (Luke 6:12) or he took Peter, James, and John with him as he went up to a mountain (Luke 9:29), Jesus modeled a healthy private life.

But it is in the privacy of the garden of Gethsemane where the depth and breadth of Jesus' soul is revealed (Matt. 26; Mark 14; Luke 22; John 17). There, as he sweat, as it were, great drops of blood, he wrestled with the ultimate purpose and responsibility of his mission. It was there that he agonized over what was before him and, with deep conviction, concluded, "Yet not what I will, but what you will."

Jesus' public ministry is also well known. We are still talking about what he said and what he did during those three short years. He often spoke of the inside condition of the heart and the outside religiosity of the religious leaders. He blasted the hypocrites who were "like whitewashed tombs" which "look beautiful on the outside but on the inside are full of the bones of the dead" (Matt. 23:27). Of them, he said, "But do not do what they do, for they do not practice what they preach" (Matt. 23:3).

The book of Acts is replete with examples of the early church praying and preaching; waiting on God and waiting on tables. Most of the Epistles have a section on doctrine in which they reference their relationship with God and a section on behavior in which they reference the far-reaching impact of their responsibility to live like the people of God.

This two-fold dimension of the private life and the public life of the people of God is just about everywhere in the Bible.

From these and many other examples a clear biblical model emerges.

THE BIBLICAL MODEL:
JOURNEY INWARD; JOURNEY OUTWARD

Years ago I heard a lecture by Dr. Loren Halvorson who framed this subject by calling it our "Journey Inward; Journey Outward." I love that designation because it eloquently captures the essence of these two realities.

When I read in the Bible of the private side of the public person in Psalms 63:8, "I cling to you," or Exodus 33:18, "Show me your glory," or Psalms 38:22, "Come quickly to help me, my Lord and my Savior," or Psalms 42:1–2, "As the deer pants for steams of water, so my soul pants for you, my God. My soul thirsts for God, for the living God," all I want to do is "go hide myself" to get on my knees and seek the face of God.

When I read the writings of pietists like J. I. Packer in his classic *Knowing God*[2] or Richard Foster's *Celebration of Discipline*[3] or Henri Nouwen's *The Wounded Healer*[4] or John Piper's *Desiring God*[5] or Gordon MacDonald's *Ordering Your Private World*,[6] I want to rent a monastery for a while to get alone with God, away from my cellphone and computer and all distractions.

Then I read in the Bible about the public side of the private person in 2 Corinthians 12:15 (KJV), "I will very gladly spend and be spent for you," or Mark 10:45 (KJV), "For even the Son of man came not to be ministered unto, but to minister, and give his life a ransom for many," or Matthew 9:37, "The harvest is plentiful but the workers are few," and I want to roll up my sleeves and get close to those in need and pour my life out as a living sacrifice doing my part to help mend broken people.

Then I read the books of activists like Elton Trueblood's *The Company of the Committed*[7] or Leonard Sweet's *I Am a Follower*[8] or Dr. James O. Davis' *How to Make Your Net Work*[9] or John Maxwell's 21 *Irrefutable Laws of Leadership*,[10] and I want to rent a communications satellite to be involved in shouting to the world the good news of the gospel.

The greatest challenge of life and leadership is the question, ***How do I balance my public life and my private life?*** How do I live my journey inward and my journey outward simultaneously?

The following circles illustrate the forces at work with our journey inward and our journey outward.

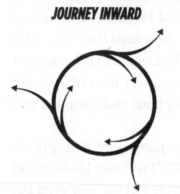

JOURNEY INWARD   **JOURNEY OUTWARD**

Consider the first circle as your Journey Inward. Imagine it going round and round clockwise, faster and faster. The faster it goes, two forces emerge: centripetal and centrifugal. With greater speed, imagine a centripetal force pulling everything toward the center of the Journey Inward circle with an equally greater force.

Simultaneously, as that Journey Inward circle goes round and round clock wise, faster and faster, imagine a centrifugal force pulling everything away from the center of the circle with an equally greater force.

Those two gravitational forces illustrate the two powerful Journey Inward forces that are always going on in our lives. The more we spend time with God and seek his face, the more we want to keep spending time with God and seeking his face. Our desire grows more and more. We hunger and thirst in new ways to experience his presence and glory. At the same time, the more we experience of him, the more it thrusts us out to want to share it with others. These centripetal and centrifugal forces grow greater the more we cultivate our Journey Inward.

Now consider the second circle as your Journey Outward. Imagine it going round and round counter-clockwise, faster and faster. The faster it goes, two forces also emerge: centripetal and centrifugal. With greater speed, imagine the centripetal force pulling everything toward the center of the Journey Outward circle with an equally greater force.

Simultaneously, as that Journey Outward circle goes round and round counter-clockwise, faster and faster, imagine a centrifugal force pulling everything away from the Journey Outward circle with an equally greater force.

Those two gravitational forces represent the two powerful Journey Outward forces that are always going on in our lives. The more we serve those who are in need and spend time with them, the more intensely we want to serve even more those who are in need and spend more time with them. At the same time, we realize how dependent we are on God and how critical it is that we spend more time with him to acquire the divine help to help others.

For me, this is one of the greatest challenges on my leadership journey. I know I must be balanced in my Journey Inward and my Journey Outward, but the tug of war to avoid a schizophrenic life is relentless. Often, I am given to one extreme or the other. The simultaneous obligatory demands of the market place and the sanctuary can pull me apart.

I return to the illustration that Dr. Halverson used in his lecture. He described the three-story-high pendulum in the science museum. Moved by the forces of gravity and the rotation of the earth, that pendulum goes back and forth, back and forth, making gentle ∞'s on the floor. With the secure anchor point at the top of the pendulum, the movement for one side or the other could never become extreme. With each movement the pendulum maintained an impeccable balance.

As we listened we immediately identified with his application when he said, "With our anchor thoroughly established in God, we will always have the capacity for balance between our Journey Inward and our Journey Outward."

JOURNEY INWARD   **JOURNEY OUTWARD**

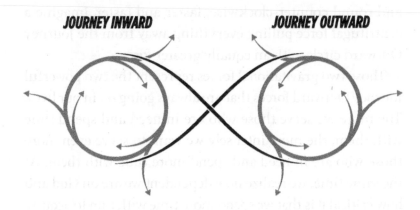

There is a holy tension between our Journey Inward and our Journey Outward. The forces seem to contradict each other but, in reality, they complement each other. Like the taunt strings on the violin, there would be no music if there were no tension. The music of our lives emerges from that holy tension.

Some of my favorite authors address this balance. Henri Nouwen's *In the Name of Jesus* observes that there are far too many followers of Jesus with "an increasing split between their own most private inner world and the good news they announce. When spirituality becomes spiritualization life in the body becomes carnality. When ministers live their ministry mostly in their heads and relate the Gospel as a set of valuable ideas to be announced, the body (of Christ) quickly takes revenge by screaming loudly for affection and intimacy."[11]

Elton Trueblood says, "The pietist needs action and the activist needs piety. Each is a half man, made such by unnecessary acts of self-limitation and consequent impoverishment—the best leaders are both service-oriented and Christ-centered. The church is never more relevant than when it is most reverent. The church is never more reverent than when it is most relevant."[12]

In *The Active Life*, Parker J. Palmer speaks of "Our Contemplative Action" and "Our Active Contemplation."[13] Both of them are essential.

As I look back on my formal and informal education, however, most of it has been to enhance my Journey Outward. I have taken classes to learn how to communicate and others to learn how to administrate. Whether it was learning to relate to different cultures or think more clearly or even to understand biblical truth or science or history or theology, the primary objectives were to help equip me for my Journey Outward.

There's no question that those skills and techniques and tools are necessary. We can never really have enough of them. Throughout our entire lives we need to keep growing in our Journey Outward. That quest never ends. No matter how high the quality of our character may become, it still doesn't necessarily mean it will make us better golfers or musicians or leaders. Competence is needed.

How do I balance my private life and my public life?
Rather than focus on our Journey Outward and what we
need to do there, the rest of this chapter will focus on our
Journey Inward. My purpose for doing it this way is to help
counter-balance the overwhelming tendency we have in leadership development to focus on what we are doing rather than
on who we are becoming.

My bookshelves are filled with books on our Journey
Outward. They are easy to find. A quick glance at the latest
leadership seminars and conferences affirms this reality. Even
the tsunami of resources on church planting seems to focus
more on church-planting techniques than on the church
planter. We obviously need all of these things, but unless we
balance our Journey Outward and Journey Inward, we will
soon find ourselves running on empty.

If David O. McKay is accurate that "The greatest battles
of life are fought out in the silent chambers of the soul," (our
Journey Inward) how can we cultivate that part of our lives?

CULTIVATING OUR JOURNEY INWARD
AND JOURNEY OUTWARD

Peter Kuzmic said, "Charisma without character leads to
catastrophe." How can we cultivate our Journey Inward?
When I read the pietists on this subject I do not find much
new material. Most of it I already know but as I digest their
meditations, the very process seeps deeper into my soul and
empowers my resolve to keep growing on my Journey Inward.

Their insights nourish my soul like spiritual comfort food. Even if I have eaten it before and no matter how much I keep growing on my Journey Inward, my roots always need to go deeper. In other words, we need more to be reminded than to be informed.

Take Control of the Calendar. Paul Rees was once asked, "How does one cultivate an intimate relationship with God?" To which he replied, "Take time to pray—you get time by making time. You prioritize. If the cultivation of an intimate life with Christ is really important to you, you organize and arrange your agenda so there is time for quietness and openness."

Unless we take control of the calendar with this priority, our Journey Outward will always dominate. I will never forget the bold statement of Dr. Robert E. Cooley to a group of Christian educators on the value of prayer when he said, "If you are not going to pray, then at least hire someone to do it."

J. Oswald Sanders said, "Leaders are qualified in secret." From our daily quiet time to an annual personal retreat, it's impossible to cultivate our Journey Inward unless we take control of our calendar and build in this priority. In *The Circle Maker* Mark Batterson said, "Prayer is the difference between the best you can do and the best God can do."

Few questions humble us more than, *How is your prayer life?* I would far rather tell you how things are going at the University of Valley Forge or with my family or what books I'm reading than to answer that question.

If we are going to cultivate our Journey Inward, we must take control of the calendar.

Learn to Be Quiet. We live in a noisy world. Try going through one day and identify all of the noises that bombard your senses. Like those loud conversations next to us in a restaurant that make it almost impossible to carry on a conversation with our dinner guests, the loud noises all around us make it almost impossible to carry on a conversation with God.

Psalms 46:10 says, "Be still, and know that I am God." Stillness. Silence. Solitude. I think sometimes God would say to us, "Shhh. No words. No music. No noise. Just be still and know me." Even in Revelation there was silence for the space of about one half hour (Rev. 8:1). That doesn't seem like very long, but what if there were a half hour silence in the middle of a symphony?

Robert Lawrence Smith wrote a little book titled *A Quaker Book of Wisdom*. The first chapter is titled "Silence" and the first sentence is, "Even pronouncing the word violates its meaning."[14] All of the Christian pietists talk about silence.

Richard Foster, "Without silence there is no solitude."

Teresa of Avila, "Settle yourself in solitude and you will come upon Him in yourself."

Morton T. Kelsey, "The first step in finding…contact with God is learning to be alone and quiet. This is the beginning of silence."

Catherine Doherty, "All in me is silent. I am immersed in the silence of God."

John Climacus, "The lover of silence draws close to God."

Meister Eckhart, "There is nothing in the world that resembles God as much as silence."

Just meditating on those words quiets my spirit. In *Dark Night of the Soul*, St. John of the Cross says twice, "My house now being stilled."[15] He never would have survived the dark night without silence.

If we are going to cultivate our Journey Inward, we must learn to be quiet.

Make Yourself Accountable. An oxymoron is a figure of speech which produces an incongruous, seemingly self-contradictory effect like "cruel kindness" or "make haste slowly" or "jumbo shrimp" or "tough love." Another oxymoron is "accountable entrepreneur."

Here our greatest strength can become our greatest weakness. The more we grow our Journey Outward gifts, the less inclined we become to allow people to hold us accountable on our Journey Inward. Years ago I had to confront a gifted leader for slippage he allowed in his public leadership influence. Though the confrontation was difficult for me, I was responsible for his performance as his supervisor. But I will never forget his reply, "What right do you have to talk to me about my performance?"

What a sad day that was for him (and me) because he refused to allow himself to be accountable. His great strength with his Journey Outward gifts clouded his awareness of his Journey Inward needs.

If we are going to cultivate our Journey Inward, we must be willing to allow ourselves to be accountable.

Stay in the Book. Deuteronomy 5:1, "Hear O Israel the decrees and laws I declare in your hearing. Learn them." God is all for Bible memorization. The religious leaders of Jesus' day went astray. Jesus told them, "You are in error because you do not know the scriptures."

The Psalmist declares his love for God's Word ten times in Psalms 119 but captures his sentiments most eloquently with "Oh how I love your law." He goes on to say he meditates on it, fears it, delights in it, hopes in it, longs for it, learns it, teaches it, keeps it, and is quickened by it.

A professional chef can starve to death serving food to others. Just being around food and smelling the rich aroma as we serve it to others doesn't feed us. For those in church vocational ministry, this kind of spiritual starvation is easier to happen than we think. It can sneak up on us as we spend more and more time preparing the public messages for our Journey Outward.

I remember what it took to prepare four original messages each week during my seven pastoral years. From the Wednesday evening Bible study to the Sunday morning adult Sunday School class to the Sunday morning and Sunday evening sermons, I must admit that sometimes I felt like I was a preaching and teaching machine. All of that was further complicated by my need to be bivocational.

During those years I had to work constantly at reading and studying the Bible because I was looking for teaching and preaching material. It was only God's frequent conviction that kept me from starving to death as I served spiritual food to others. I loved being the spiritual chef serving others the food, but even to this day, I always find it challenging and must be ever deliberate to take the necessary time to sit down and be fed spiritually myself.

If we are going to cultivate our Journey Inward, we must be willing to stay in the Book.

Stay in Your Books. Here is one of the saddest remarks I ever heard from a college graduate after he left his alma mater, "I haven't read a book in ten years and I don't intend to." With the avalanche of digital materials, fewer and fewer leaders cultivate reading as part of their Journey Inward.

My books are my friends. I write in them. I like to hold them. I even like to smell them. There is nothing like the smell of a new book—or an old one. I love to breathe in everything I can from my books.

Mark Twain is credited with saying something like, "A person who can read and doesn't has no advantage over he who can't read at all."

If you've never thought about forming a personal philosophy of reading, I would encourage you to consider it to help you cultivate your Journey Inward. (I'll address this more in the next chapter.) My reading revolves around three primary areas: devotional/spiritual; leadership; academic. If you were to walk into my office you would find evidence of these priorities everywhere on my bookshelves.

I love to ask my friends, "Have you read any good books lately?" The answer to that question has sent me on many missions to find new "friends."

If we are going to cultivate our Journey Inward, we must be willing to read. Whether you are reading from your Kindle or your book—read.

Change the Subject. For many years, J. Philip Hogan was the leader of the Assemblies of God missionary movement. His influence around the world was legendary. Those of us who knew him are still telling stories about him.

During one of his messages when he was sharing a challenge about the greatness of the harvest and how important it was that we make ourselves available to follow the call of God wherever it might lead, he told something from his personal life that actually startled me.

He loved horses. And because of that love, he joined the Sheriff's Posse where he lived in Springfield, Missouri. From time to time there were those who criticized him because they felt that riding his horse was a waste of his time. They thought he should be giving all of his time to eternal matters, to which he said, "Even a missionary can't be a missionary all the time." From time to time, even J. Philip Hogan needed to change the subject in his life.

No matter what you do and no matter how important it is, sometimes you must just get out of town. Evie and I love to drive about an hour west of where we live. As we meander through the small roads with Amish farms on each side, this farm boy with his city girl beside him breathe in that fresh country air. Our spirits are renewed because we get out of the routines.

I guess that's why I love growing flowers in our country garden. For me, growing vegetables is too much like the vegetable garden we had on our farm as I was growing up. Working that garden was *work*. But no matter how hard I work, tending my flower garden renews my soul.

Photography does the same for me. Every time I look through my camera I go to another place.

Please don't misunderstand me. I like to be where I am. I like to be in the present moment. But there are just times when we all need a change, even if only for an hour or two.

Even a walk outside over lunch can contribute greatly to our Journey Inward.

If we are going to cultivate our Journey Inward, every now and then we must change the subject.

Cultivate the Personal Disciplines. When I first read Richard Foster's *Celebration of Discipline,* his words influenced me for more than a decade. Hearing him at a workshop and then meeting him for breakfast around that time solidified my admiration for his writing.

I still remember his opening words, "Superficiality is the curse of our age. The doctrine of instant satisfaction is a primary spiritual problem. The desperate need today is not for a greater number of intelligent or gifted people but for deep people." His list of Inward disciplines (Meditation; Prayer; Fasting; Study), Outward Disciplines (Simplicity; Solitude; Submission; Service), and Corporate Disciplines (Confession; Worship; Guidance; Celebration) still challenge me.[16]

If we are going to cultivate our Journey Inward, we can never get away from cultivating the personal disciplines.

Cultivate a Hunger and Thirst for God. When we get sick, our appetite usually goes first. We can walk in front of an all-you-can-eat smorgasbord but nothing appeals to us if we are not well.

In one of Vance Havner's little books that compiles his sermons, he begins by telling the story of a group of people who were traveling on a train across the Great Plains in the middle of February. The view out the window was anything but inspiring. Everyone was bored to death except for one man on the train.

As he looked out the window he was obviously awed by what he saw. Again and again sounds of amazement and surprise filled the railroad car.

Finally someone could take the curiosity no longer. The person just had to know why this man seemed to be having the time of his life when everyone else couldn't wait for the trip to be over. Someone finally got enough courage to ask him why he was so different from the rest of them and what he was seeing that they were not.

He replied, "Until a few days ago, I was blind. And a famous surgeon on the East Coast performed a delicate surgery and restored my eyesight. So, I guess what you are seeing is common place, but for me it is out of this world."

The title of Vance Havner's sermon is "Have You Lost the Wonder?" How easy it's to lose the wonder of what it means to follow Jesus. Without that wonder, every part of our journey, whether it is the Journey Inward or the Journey Outward, loses its value.

Keith Miller wrote a book years ago titled *The Becomers*.[17] I love that title because it captures the essence of Jesus' words in Mark 1:17 (KJV), "Come ye after me and I will make you to become fishers of men." Unless we are hungry and thirsty to become what God wants us to become, we will never become what God wants us to be. We will become something less.

If you are going to cultivate your Journey Inward, you must maintain your hunger and thirst.

Give Yourself Time. None of us can ignore the law of agriculture. No matter how hard we try, if we plant corn in August there will never be a harvest in September. The microwave oven does not work in the field.

In *The Circle Maker*, Mark Batterson said, "We over-estimate what we can do in two years and we under-estimate what we can do in 10 years."[18] Abraham waited twenty-five years for God to fulfill his promise. Jacob was a long time becoming Israel. Joseph was seventeen years old when he had his dreams and it was over twenty years later until his brothers bowed down before him. And David did not go from the pasture to the palace in one step.

Time can sour us. Time can discourage us. Time can embitter us. Time equalizes. Time creates. Time produces. Time builds. Time develops. Time changes. No wonder when his cause was shot down in the British Parliament, Gladstone gave these parting words, "I appeal to time."

Often some time is required between the moment one speaks to the mountain and when it finally disappears into the sea. The farmer plows, plants, waters, then waits, waits, waits, waits, waits, then harvests.

If you are going to cultivate your Journey Inward, you must think like a farmer.

Share What You Receive with Others. As we learn to cultivate our Journey Inward, we must never lose the perspective that the intent is also to enhance our Journey Outward. Remember, the Jordan River dies at the Dead Sea. Everything flows in and nothing flows out. The Dead Sea is rich with minerals, but it's void of life. It cannot sustain marine life due to more than 25 percent of the content being minerals. Living waters must keep flowing (Journey Outward).

The goal of cultivating our Journey Inward is not to acquire more, but to acquire more so we can share more. Otherwise, we become stale, stagnant, in-grown and self-absorbed. And we find ourselves agreeing with the person who said, "Most of us act at some time or other as though we are at the center of the universe—and are irritated when most of the rest of the population pretends they have not gotten the memo."

If you're going to cultivate your Journey Inward, you must be prepared to share with others everything that you have received for yourself.

CONCLUSION

The question of this chapter is, ***How do I balance my public life and my private life?*** So where are you on your journey? It's impossible to make good decisions in public if we have not become good people in private. Mark Wilson is a great example. Mark Wilson is an honest man. His decision to dock himself two strokes at the 2007 Honda Classic will be forever remembered as one of the great acts of honesty in professional golf. He was struggling to make the cut in Palm Beach Gardens, Florida. He needed three routine shots to finish the par-3 fifth hole on his second round.

Unfortunately, Chris Jones, Wilson's caddie, told Camilo Villegas, who was playing aside Wilson, what club his boss had used on that hole. And that's where Rule 8-1 applied.

Giving another player any advice during competition is strictly prohibited. Wilson knew it was wrong and he knew he would pay dearly for his caddie's mistake. On the sixth tee he called a rules official and docked himself two strokes. That simple act of honesty placed his chances of staying for the weekend in serious jeopardy.

"I thought we were done," the caddie said.

In an amazing turnaround, Wilson shot eight under par on the next forty-nine holes, which tied him with three other golfers for a playoff. He ultimately won his first tour victory, earning him a $990,000 check.

That gesture of honesty now forever identifies that rule as "The Mark Wilson Rule." Can you imagine how Wilson would have felt if he had been dishonest and won the tournament? Every time he looked at his trophy or spent his money, deep in his heart he would have known he didn't really earn it.

You just don't grow character like that by accident. It requires a vigilant attention to our Journey Inward.

In *Leadership,* the popular journal for Christian leaders, the editor interviewed David and Helen Seamands regarding the challenges they had faced in ministry. Toward the end of the article David was asked if he had ever aspired to climb the denominational ladder in the United Methodist Church. When I first read his words I was deeply moved and they continue to speak to me over thirty years later.

"No, I remember a crisis with this on the mission field. We were stuck in an out-of-the-way place during a record monsoon; it had rained for 56 straight days. You couldn't go out, and I did a lot of thinking: 'Here I am in the middle of nowhere wasting my life. With all my great talents, this is absurd.' The voice of the Spirit spoke to me very clearly, 'David, if you stay in this isolated village the rest of your life, that is not your business. Your job is to take care of the depth of your ministry. My job is to take care of the breadth of your ministry. If I want to spread you around, that's my work. You just dig down deeper.' That was a turning point for me in terms of life planning."[19]

With relentless demands, our tasks keep coming at us. Keeping up with them is similar to that old *I Love Lucy* television episode where the conveyor with candy goes faster and faster and there's just no way that Lucy can keep up. On occasion Evie will ask me if I am caught up with my to-do list and I always answer the same way, "I am never caught up. There is always more to do than I have time to do."

But I have learned over the years that leadership is much like farming. You will never hear a farmer say, "I am done." Farmers just stop for the day. The challenge for the farmer is the same challenge for everyone who has too much to do and not enough time to do it, *When should I stop? What can I put off until tomorrow? How can I balance my life?*

How do I balance my private life and my public life? The more we can understand the holy tension between our Journey Inward and our Journey Outward, the more likely we will find balance in our private life and our public life.

The stakes are huge. As Phillips Brooks said, "Someday in the years to come, you will be wrestling with the great temptation, or trembling under the great sorrow of your life. But the real struggle is here—now. Now is being decided whether, in the day of your supreme sorrow or temptation, you shall miserably fail or gloriously conquer. Character cannot be made except by a long and steady process."

My friend Roland Dudley said it like this, "To do a Jesus kind of work requires a Jesus kind of person."

CHAPTER 8

How Do I Keep Growing as a Leader?

*You've got to do your own growing, no
matter how tall your grandfather was.*
Irish Proverb

*My mother said to me, "If you become a soldier, you'll be
a general; if you become a monk, you'll end up as Pope."
Instead, I became a painter and wound up as Picasso.*
Pablo Picasso

*The main interest in life and work is to become
someone else that you were not in the beginning.*
Michael Foucault

I heard a hilarious story about a first grader named Brandon who tried to build his muscles during a Saturday evening bath. After he had finished his bath, his mother, Susan, went to drain the tub and noticed that all of the shampoo was gone from a brand-new bottle. She thought it was a little odd but just dismissed it from her mind.

Later that evening Brandon was in his pajamas and acted a little strange as his parents walked into the living room. His father, Steve, described the scene, "He kept staring at his biceps and giggling. So we giggled too. Sometimes just watching a six-year-old acting weird can make you laugh."

"Son, what's so funny?" Steve asked. Brandon said, "Do my muscles look any bigger?"

His dad responded, "Well, they look a little bigger" (although in reality they were still the lanky arms of a first grader). Brandon laughed some more causing his dad to ask him again, "What's so funny?"

With that Brandon said, "Come here," and took his dad to the bathroom where he picked up the empty bottle of shampoo, which shared some insight into why his son was acting so strange. "Dad, I took this whole bottle of shampoo and put it all over my body. I am feeling a lot bigger. Can you tell? See it says right here: 'BODY BUILDING FORMULA!'"

Steve said he thought he was going to slip a disk he laughed so hard. Brandon assumed you could shortcut certain laws of nature to achieve preferred results. No matter how hard we try, some laws cannot be broken and if we try to break them, we discover they break us. No matter how positive our attitude or who we know or how invincible we may seem, a jump from a tall building will not defy the law of gravity.

In *Zorba, the Greek* Nikos Kazantzakis tells a tale about the way even well-intentioned efforts can cause real harm.[1] His character once discovered a cocoon in the bark of a tree just as a butterfly was making a hole in the case to come out. Growing impatient, the observer blew on it to warm it, desiring to help the process. But to the horror of the helper, the butterfly came out with its wings folded back and crumpled.

That warm breath caused the butterfly to appear before its time and in a different way and, in spite of a desperate struggle, it died in the palm of the very hand that had tried to help it.

Kazantzakis wisely concluded, "It is a mortal sin to violate the great laws of nature."

I love to watch things grow. I would love to take you for a walk in my flower garden. We live in Chester County in an old 1850s farmhouse, a perfect place to have a country garden. I've been working at mine since 1997. With sweat clouding my glasses I have often thought, "Without a gardener, there would be no garden."

I enjoy the work of gardening, but I also enjoy the results of gardening. Each day, I observe something new in my garden. As the seasons change, so does my garden. The colors, shapes and sizes, angles, textures, odors, and tastes declare their silent messages about growth.

On just one day in late summer, I tasted mint tea and smelled the leaves of monarda. I looked at the last dahlias and roses of the season. I saw the remains of brilliant coreopsis and black-eyed Susans with their seeds that will start another season next spring. I received the beauty of wisteria, peonies, hydrangea, coleus, zinnias, mums, liatris, daylilies, red raspberries, butterfly bushes, zebra grasses, hostas, ferns, and Jerusalem artichokes. Each plant tells me something unique about its growth.

Whether we ponder the growth of muscles, insects, flowers, or leaders, many of the same principles apply. If you want to grow as a leader, there are some laws that God has created which we avoid at our own peril.

It would, obviously, be impossible here to address all of the growth needs of every leader. That would be unrealistic. We

want to keep before us, however, this most important question of how a leader keeps growing. Leaders must consider
all areas of growth, particularly those that God highlights.

To begin answering this question, Jesus is our perfect
model of growth for all leaders.

We know very little of the early years of Jesus' life. Alfred
Edersheim in *The Life and Times of Jesus the Messiah* said,
"There is something grand, even awful, in the absolute silence
which lies upon the 30 years between the birth and the first
Messianic manifestations of Jesus."[2]

We do get some early glimpses in the gospels of Matthew,
Mark, and John, but it's Luke who opens the window the
most. Luke 2:40 probably summarizes his first twelve years,
"And the child grew and became strong; he was filled with
wisdom, and the grace of God was on him." Luke 2:52 likely
is a summary of the subsequent eighteen years, "And Jesus
grew in wisdom and stature, and in favor with God and man."

According to Mark 6:3, he grew up in a fairly large family.
In the Gospels and according to the early church fathers, there
are allusions that his stepfather, Joseph, died early. Jesus was
a carpenter and in those days carpentry included masonry.
He would have routinely built houses and made all kinds of
furniture, including household and agriculture items like
ploughs and yokes.

The word *grew* in Luke 2:52 also means *increased* or literally
to cut in front. Jesus was cutting his way forward as though
he were going through a jungle or forest like a pioneer. He
led the way and was perfect at each stage of his development.
He demonstrated well-rounded growth.

We learn from Jesus' example that he grew through every stage of his life. But in Luke 2, it's the beginning that is documented. The beginning is always important. As Plato said, "You know also the beginning is the most important part of every work, especially in the case of a young and tender thing; for that is the time at which the character is being formed and the desired impression is more readily given."

If we are going to answer the question, *How can I grow as a leader?* it will help us to understand the question, *How did Jesus grow as a leader?*

JESUS GREW IN WISDOM
(INTELLECTUALLY)

Jesus' growth involved more than just learning information. He grew in knowledge, which includes wisdom. At age twelve he amazed the religious leaders of the day. After three days of looking for him, they found him "in the temple courts, sitting among the teachers, listening to them and asking them questions. Everyone who heard him was amazed at his understanding and his answers" (Luke 2:46–47).

Anyone who studies his illustrations and conversations realizes he was an outstanding communicator. Those earthly stories with heavenly meanings (the parables) had a way of sneaking up on the listeners and, just when they were wide open to the stories, he made his spiritual and poignant point. He could talk to lawyers and widows, religious leaders and tax collectors, huge crowds and individuals. His questions pierced to the heart of the most critical cynic.

How can I grow as a leader? The mind of Jesus is exemplary for anyone who asks that question. Intellectually, he was perfectly developed at each stage in his life, including this one.

That billboard on the side of the road in Minneapolis said it all, "Christ died to take away our sins, not our minds."

The title of Mark Noll's book *The Scandal of the Evangelical Mind* captured the attention of a lot of people but nothing like the first sentence of his book did: "The scandal of the evangelical mind is that there is not much of an evangelical mind."[3]

His words challenge every leader to grow intellectually, "The search for a Christian perspective on life—in our families, our economies, our leisure activities, our sports, our attitudes to the care of the body and health care, our reactions to novels and paintings, as well as our churches and our specifically Christian activities—is not just an academic exercise. The effort to think like a Christian is rather an effort to take seriously the sovereignty of God over the world He created, the lordship of Christ over the world He died to redeem, and the power of the Holy Spirit over the world He sustains each and every moment."

As I mentioned earlier, I never planned to go to college. In high school I joined the FFA (Future Farmers of America). I enjoyed learning but it was not a passion of my life. Formal education didn't seem all that important for me as a dairy farmer.

But with my father's death and God's call to ministry, I found my way into a college classroom. The advice a mentor gave me changed my entire life, "The time you take to sharpen your tools is never wasted."

Quickly I learned that I had much to learn. My classes introduced me to worlds I never knew existed. During my first trip home someone asked me what I had learned so far and I still remember my answer, "I learned how little I know."

Most of the sermons I preached before I had Homiletics were mush; some of the nutrients were there but nothing was very well organized. Communication skills came slowly. At times I wanted to say to those who heard me, "I know that you believe you understand what you think I said, but I'm not sure you realize that what you heard isn't really what I meant." I had a lot to learn—that became very obvious to this former farm boy.

But I was committed to keep growing intellectually. God had called me to lead and I had to discover a strategy to fuel my intellectual growth. It was during those years and since that I developed a philosophy of reading. Nothing I have ever done over the years has helped me grow intellectually more than that.

In 2 Timothy 4:9–13 Paul makes an important request, "Do your best to come to me quickly. ...When you come, bring the cloak that I left with Carpus at Troas and my scrolls, especially the parchments." Charles Spurgeon understood why Paul needed his books when he observed, "Even an apostle must read. He is inspired and yet he wants books. He has seen the Lord and yet he wants books. He has been caught up into the third heaven and had heard things which it was unlawful for a man to utter, yet he wants books."

Leaders must master the art of reading if we are going to grow intellectually.

You may ask me, "Why do you read?" I read for all kinds of reasons. Obviously, I read to help me continue growing and because it is a necessary obligation. Leaders must read. Nothing will slow down your leadership development more than not reading.

But I also read because I want to. Sometimes I read something just because I'm curious about it. If I'm traveling to a new place, I try to pick up at least a book or two to prepare me for everything I will face. From poetry to life in East Africa and from storytelling to World War II, there are just so many wonderful and fascinating things to learn.

There are even times I pick something up to read just because it's enjoyable. I once found this little book on *Southern Mountain Humor* in a bookstore in Lexington, Kentucky. I could hardly put it down. Robert Frost's poems remind me of the farm and Paul Harvey's *For What It's Worth* made me realize that truth really is stranger than fiction.

Lest you think I always have a book in my hands, there are reasons why I don't read. Most of us can't stop life in order to read a book. Family time and recreational time always invite me to read later. Life must also be balanced. I love my books but not more than those around me. There are times when I am just too tired to read. Yes, I have even fallen asleep with my Bible in my hands.

There are some things I read daily, weekly, monthly, and annually (like when I am on vacation or during the busy but change-of-routine summer). I read newspapers, news magazines, and all kinds of journals. I am usually reading several books simultaneously, in the three areas of personal development I previously mentioned: devotional/spiritual, leadership, and academic.

A few suggestions for developing a reading strategy:

- Be selective. Skim some books; skip others.
- Read slowly. Some books are not to be read hurriedly.
- Read a little at a time. I remember reading *Les Miserables*. It took me a long time, but page by page I did it.
- Read what interests you. Why take time to read something that doesn't interest you or what doesn't speak to the goals and demands that matter to you?
- Go from easy to harder. Start with the easy and work your way up from there.
- Ask others what they're reading. Their interests will help you find many new literary friends.
- Be willing to browse catalogs, libraries, and bestseller lists. Ideas can come from anywhere.
- Don't be afraid to say no. People have recommended many books to me and, once I started them, I discover they're just not the kind I want to read. And even if someone gives you a book to read, it doesn't mean you have to read it.

Sometimes I encounter someone who tells me they don't like to read. If that's where you find yourself, you MUST do something about it. John Wesley told younger ministers of the Wesleyan Societies either to read or get out of the ministry.

If you don't like to read, these suggestions may help.

- Pray for God's help. The Holy Spirit will guide you into all truth.
- Make sure you settle in your heart why you should read. Establishing your rationale and then going from there will do more for your problem with reading than anything else.
- Start with the simple and the enjoyable. Even if you begin with children's books, start reading something.
- Get to know your authors. If you get the opportunity to meet the author of a book, it can help make reading it much more dynamic. You'll hear and feel that author on the pages.
- Read with a friend. This doesn't work for me, but it does work for some. It helps with accountability.
- Read Mortimer Adler's *How to Read a Book*.[4] This sounds contradictory. Why suggest reading a book about reading a book if reading is the problem? Well, if you can muster up the initiative to read this one, I promise it will help you as you read all other books.
- Acquire the skill of speed-reading. Take a class or find out about it. It doesn't make reading seem so intimidating.
- Don't be intimidated by someone else who loves to read. If you like to read, even a little, at least start with that.

Jesus grew in wisdom. Learning to read well will be one of the most powerful ways you will grow in wisdom.

JESUS GREW IN STATURE
(PHYSICALLY)

Our second trip to Israel was much better than our first one. The second time we didn't even drive by a hospital! But during that trip we were able to visit the places I had studied and taught about. My pictures don't begin to capture it all. Besides, taking a picture of someone riding a camel is not the same as getting on one.

I now understand more of what Jesus' "growth in stature" must have meant. Because Jesus was not taken by limousine or airplane from place to place, his physical condition had to be better than most of ours today. When Jesus went "up to Jerusalem," the elevation and terrain were enough to develop his cardiovascular system. Traveling to Caesarea Philippi all the way in the northern part of Israel could not be done without huge effort. We read of him on the Mount of Transfiguration, traveling through the Jordan River valley, being thrust out into the desert and even going through the unwelcomed region of Samaria.

Jesus endured the rigors of walking the hot, parched, and rugged countryside of that crossroads land between three continents. He didn't just sit under a shade tree in one place waiting for people to come to him. He went to them even though the physical demands to reach them were enormous.

Life-giving water was precious. Accommodations were limited. Travel in the ancient world during Jesus' day was anything but easy. But because Jesus "grew in stature," he was capable of enduring the harshest conditions.

How can I grow as a leader? Jesus growth in stature is a model for us.

Did you know that each year the USA spends several trillion dollars on health care and health-related items? And, according to experts, preventable illness makes up approximately 80 percent of the burden of illness and 90 percent of all hospital care. Most of us know what to do; we just don't do it.

For most leaders, it is easier to talk about financial stewardship than the stewardship of our bodies. It's even easier to talk about various dimensions of how to live as followers of Jesus than the stewardship of our bodies. When leaders bring up this subject, the room usually gets very quiet. Mark Twain's comment is probably part of the reason, "Nothing so needs reforming as much as other people's habits." If you are going to be an effective leader, then a strategy to grow in stature must be part of your life.

Different seasons of my life have necessitated different approaches to my own physical wellness. Early in my life, I didn't think about it because it just happened on the farm. From doing the chores with a dairy herd to running farm machinery all season and from planting to cultivating and from harvesting to storage, farmers work hard. They must restore energy through good food and adequate sleep or they just won't survive.

During my college years, the disciplines of the academy took over. Physical education classes and intramural sports kept me on the move. I especially loved playing shortstop on my college softball team. During the summers I always returned home to work on the farm. I also played softball on our church softball team. During those years, my physical activities were quite regular.

Once I graduated from college and our children came along, the routines of my life changed. I had to be much more intentional about maintaining my exercise routines. During our early years in Minnesota, I got up early in the morning to run in the gymnasium. Even though I tried other shoes and changed my running style, I still developed shin splints and had to stop. Again, my exercise habits changed.

Then I got my first stationary bike. I literally wore one out and had to get another one. I love the stationary bike because it allows me to read while I'm biking. And that makes me always want to ride more. Even to this day, if I am riding my forty-minute regimen, I never yet have wanted to stop.

During the years when our children were in high school, there was a tennis court in the park across from our house. We still remember playing each other as darkness settled in. We listened for the ball to bounce, calling them *sound shots* because we just had to finish one more game. During those years, we were evenly matched and any one of us could have been the champion for a day.

Everything changes with age. I need more sleep than I used to. With a busier schedule today, it's harder to find time for my stationary bike. I can't eat as much. Evie and I find ourselves sharing more meals when we go out to eat.

I work harder to be flexible. Physical tasks take longer and I feel the effects more than I used to. During each season of life, I have tried to find practical opportunities that help me to be a good steward of my body.

Here are some suggestions to help you grow physically.

- Pray for wisdom to understand what it means to be a good steward of your body. We can get so busy we don't even stop to let God enlighten and help us.
- Don't let other people impose on you what works for them. Some people swim and it works for them. Exodus 15:10 describes Pharaoh and his army, but it also describes me: "They sank like lead in the mighty waters."
- Make sure you always have the blessing of your doctor. We should never begin or continue a serious health regimen without the care and guidance of health experts.
- Set realistic goals. It's not necessary to become a marathon runner in two weeks. Be patient and consistent.
- Consistency will always win. There is enormous power in little-by-little progress. We really can move the mountain a shovel at a time.
- Act your age. Just recently I played tennis with Darin and Kevin. It was not a pretty sight. We had a great time but there was no way I could even pretend to play like I used to. Yes, I did feel it the next day.
- Try something different and try it at a different time. Who knows, you might discover something new that you love and it may fit at a different time than you ever thought possible.
- Eat better. You are what you eat. Even though, like me, you may enjoy quarter pounders with cheese and large french fries from McDonald's, they should probably be the exception rather than the rule.

- Modify your routines as you move through life's seasons. But never stop. Always have a routine.

Jesus grew in stature. Learning to be a good steward of our body will greatly assist us to grow in stature.

JESUS GREW IN FAVOR WITH GOD (SPIRITUALLY)

At Jesus' baptism, the Holy Spirit descended on him as a dove and a voice came from heaven saying, "You are my Son, whom I love; with you I am well pleased" (Luke 3:22). Jesus, the Son of God, had an intimate relationship with the Father. He cultivated that intimate relationship with a prayer life that's a model for all of us to follow.

Throughout his life that intimacy marked everything he did and every part of who he was. Even as a young child, his question to his parents framed his priorities, "Didn't you know I had to be in my Father's house?"(Luke 2:49).

For Christian leaders, abundant resources are available to assist us to grow spiritually. Everywhere we look, many tools are easily within reach. Rather than list yet more things to do or even explain further ways to answer the question of how to grow spiritually, I'll instead share what I feel is the primary need we all have as leaders if we are going to grow spiritually.

At the center of all spiritual growth is our deep desire to want to grow closer to God. If that desire is lukewarm and we're satisfied where we are, spiritual growth will be virtually impossible. In the Sermon on the Mount Jesus declared, "Blessed are those who hunger and thirst for righteousness, for they will be filled" (Matt. 5:6). For most of us, being hungry means it's one o'clock and we missed lunch by an hour or so. For most of us, being thirsty means we need to reach for a bottle of water for a drink. The desperation for these life-giving necessities in Jesus' day is usually lost on us.

David said, "You, God, are my God. Earnestly I seek you; I thirst for you, my whole being longs for you, in a dry and parched land where there is no water" (Ps. 63:1). Or, "As the deer pants for streams of water, so my soul pants for you, my God" (Ps. 42:1).

Spiritual growth cannot happen without hunger and thirst like that. Or would we rather "enjoy the fleeting pleasures of sin" (Heb. 11:25)? Matt Emmons learned the hazard of aiming at the wrong target during the Summer Olympics in Athens in 2004. He had one gold medal already in the 50-meter rifle (prone position). He was assured another gold medal if he just earned a few more easy points in the three-position rifle event. He was in first place until his ninth and final shot.

He was shooting in lane two but mistakenly he fired into lane three, the target of Austria's Christian Planner. As a result, he ended up with zero on his shot and came in eighth in the competition, missing any chance of any medal.

Even if we have great hunger and thirst, what are we aiming at? Oswald Chambers said, "Beware of anything that comes with loyalty to Jesus Christ. The greatest competitor of devotion to Jesus is service for him. The one aim of the call of God is the satisfaction of God, not a call to do something for him." No wonder he loved and often repeated the phrase "Be Absolutely His."

I love Evie with all my heart. Can you imagine if I asked her, "How much can I get by with and still have you be willing to allow me to remain your husband? How close to the edge can I get and have you still tolerate my behavior?" What if a follower of Jesus asked those questions of him? We all know those are the wrong questions.

Spiritual growth will take place in direct proportion to our hunger and thirst for God. But just being in the vicinity of where God is at work is no guarantee that we will keep growing.

When I think about the importance of spiritual growth here at UVF, I'm always haunted by the stories of Samuel and the two sons of Eli, Hophni and Phinehas, in 1 Samuel 2-3. In the very same atmosphere where God was transforming the life of Samuel as he grew before the Lord, Hophni and Phinehas were falling apart before the Lord. Triumph and tragedy occurred in the same place where the glory of God was being revealed.

Sin has been described as seeing ourselves out of proportion to the universe. Twelve inches of rain can fall on concrete and it will never help to grow anything. Spiritual growth requires receptivity to what God is doing. As Anthony, one of our students, once said, "If you want to get close to God, it's on you." How tragic if here on our campus even one student missed the priceless revelation of the presence of God because he or she was more like Hophni and Phinehas than Samuel.

Jesus grew in favor with God. Every leader must have an insatiable hunger and thirst for God or spiritual growth will never happen.

JESUS GREW IN FAVOR WITH MEN
(SOCIALLY)

To understand how to grow socially, we would do well to examine the social interactions of Jesus. Jesus was welcomed at weddings and where sinners gathered. Jesus came against social injustice. He shocked his hearers by speaking of a good Samaritan (Luke 10:25–37). To those who taunted him about the woman caught in adultery he said, "Let any one of you who is without sin be the first to throw a stone at her" (John 8:7).

From "turn the other cheek" (Matt. 5:39; Luke 6:29) to "go the second mile," (Matt. 5:38–48) and from "forgive seventy times seven" (Matt. 18:22) to "those who take up the sword will perish with the sword" (Matt. 26:52), the ethics of Jesus perplexed many who heard him. Donald B. Kraybill wrote a book titled *The Upside-Down Kingdom.*[5] In it he documents this quality of Jesus' social interactions.

One of the most visible evidences of Jesus' social growth pertains to his capacity to forgive. All his life he refused to allow those who hurt him to define him. Even after all the abuse and injustice, when he was on the cross he said, "Father, forgive them, for they do not know what they are doing" (Luke 23:34).

One of the most visible evidences of social growth as leaders is to cultivate this capacity to forgive. We live in a broken world. Sin abounds. Mistakes multiply. Relationships get strained. The toast burns. The milk spills. The appointment is forgotten. The smart remark is made. The sarcastic email is sent. The phone is slammed down. The vow is broken. We turn around and walk away.

Lee Iacocca said, "Anyone who doesn't get along with people has earned the kiss of death, because that's all we've got around here are people." Thomas Merton acknowledged that very few people are sanctified in isolation. It's in community where the quality of our following Jesus is most often put to the test.

I have a friend who likes to ask missionaries to tell him about the greatest challenge they face. He has never once had one of them say it was their budget or learning a new language or even adapting to a new culture. The number one problem missionaries shared with him was missionaries getting along with other missionaries.

This brings me to what in my opinion is the greatest hindrance to effective leadership for any leader. We must learn to forgive. Deep hurts can destroy us. Pain can come at us like an avalanche and sweep everything in our lives away. Unless we have the ability to forgive and let it go, that pain will infect us like gangrene.

Early in our first year of pastoring, Evie and I faced a particular kind of pain with a person in our church. His family invited us to their home for dinner and we joyfully accepted. The meal and fellowship were wonderful. When we finished, Evie and I sat down on the couch.

Then Bob took a spiral notebook and threw it on the floor at our feet. When I opened it I read these words: "Dear Don, Eat your heart out kid." I was shocked. I quickly perused the notebook in which were thirty-two grievances against me, mostly related to questions about my motives for doing what we were doing.

Evie and I knew that was not the time to respond, so we excused ourselves as graciously as we could. We then drove a few miles away and parked our car along a small country road and there, through tears, we read the false accusations. We had no way of knowing that years later, when we were in another place of ministry, Bob would apologize for all the false things he had written and admit that he was the problem. But that night and during the days and weeks that followed our hearts were painfully broken.

Few things upset me more than being falsely accused. It's one thing to be guilty of something and have to face the music, but when it isn't true, that stabs me to the core. And when it comes from a dear friend it's hard to know what to do. As someone said, "A friend is someone who will stab you in the front."

I don't recall all that we did to process that pain in our spirits because it was a long time ago. But I do remember the powerful need to forgive that family, especially when it was the last thing we wanted to do.

Hurt and anger can conquer our spirit. An unforgiving spirit can poison everything. Our eyes see life through bitterness lenses and the shades are always dark. Over the years I've observed leaders struggle and struggle with the hurt and pain caused by people who do ungodly things against them. They have been battered by behaviors that have made their spirits numb. And as they talk about how they've been treated, you can feel the pathos in the air and you can see the pain in their eyes.

It seems as though these kinds of things are happening more and more. Our culture seems to allow adversarial vocabulary and downright obnoxious attitudes. Some people seem to delight in being cantankerous. Leaders never will please everyone. That's why people used to say, "You can always tell who the pioneers are because of the arrows in their backs." Or you hear church leaders say, "Sheep bite."

But now with social media, it seems to have reached excruciating possibilities for hurt and with the click of a keystroke, the whole world knows. Unless we learn how to forgive those within the church, we can never serve those outside the church.

Years ago one of my friends came to me and told me that a colleague had declared war on me. I still can hardly comprehend someone doing that. At first I was incredibly surprised but the more I pondered it, the more it got inside of me. I knew I would have to let it go, with God's grace. And, in time, I did.

Evie and I will never forget the deep pain that we faced on another occasion by someone we dearly loved with all our hearts. It would be impossible for me to describe the impact of that person's behavior on us. It literally stopped us in our tracks. For a year following that incident Evie said, "I feel as though grief is sitting on my soul." Even today that pain can bubble to the surface and tempt me to act unlike a follower of Jesus. Deep pain hurts deeply and requires a deep forgiveness.

The stakes are huge for all of us. If we don't get this right, nothing else will work. That's why I'm focusing on forgiveness as the primary need we have if we are to grow socially. What are you to do as a leader when you face things like that? There is hardly a greater challenge to our social growth than learning how to find a solution to this enormous problem—forgiveness.

A leader of the Warsaw ghetto uprising talked about the Holocaust and the bitterness that remained in his soul over how he and his neighbors were treated by the Nazis, "If you could lick my heart, it would poison you."

Hurt people really do hurt people. In *The Count of Monte Cristo*, Alexander Dumas eloquently tells the story of revenge.[6] And though it came for his hero, he couldn't get the bitter taste out of his mouth. We have all seen revenge ruin the good in the best and make them the worst.

The Old Testament story of Joseph is one of the great stories of forgiveness. The hurt was undeniable. His brothers betrayed him. The effects were irreversible. Joseph never could get those years back. Revenge seemed justifiable. Those brothers saw how distressed he was when he pleaded with them for his life but they would not listen. But it was all forgivable. His paradigm was different.

The story of Desmond Tutu is also a great story of forgiveness. When apartheid was abolished in South Africa, the overwhelming majority of the country's inhabitants could only envision two possible scenarios. One was to provide general amnesty for everyone by forgetting all the crimes committed during this dark period in history, as if nothing ever happened. The other was to use the judicial system and through a systematic and methodical effort, bring charges and/or imprisonment for all the crimes that had been committed.

Desmond Tutu said the first option was unacceptable and the second option was impractical. He proposed a third option. He said, "We cannot forget. We cannot bring justice. But we can forgive." He went on to say that forgiveness is not forgetting. Forgiveness means listening to every detail of everything a victim suffered, as expressed by the perpetrators, and then renouncing the idea of revenge.

No wonder he won the Nobel Peace Prize.

Robert D. Enright has been called "The Father of Forgiveness Research." He is a professor of Educational Psychology at the University of Wisconsin-Madison and president of the International Forgiveness Institute. He lists five things that forgiveness is not:[7]

1. **Forgetting.** Deep hurts can rarely be wiped out of one's awareness. We actually never have to forgive and forget because if forgiving requires forgetting, we probably never could forgive.
2. **Reconciliation.** Reconciliation takes two people; but an injured party can forgive an offender without reconciliation.
3. **Condoning.** Forgiveness does not necessarily excuse bad or hurtful behavior.
4. **Dismissing.** Forgiveness involves taking the offense seriously, not passing it off as inconsequential or insignificant.
5. **Pardoning.** A pardon is a legal transaction that releases the offender from the consequences of an action, such as a penalty. Forgiveness is a personal transaction that releases the one offended from the offense.

I have found Enright's list to be an enormous help as I've struggled with forgiveness. Actually, this list is extremely liberating. It also helps me as I minister to those who are working through their own personal challenges with forgiveness. Sometimes our opinion of forgiveness is based on an inaccurate understanding of what forgiveness really is.

If I were to describe what forgiveness is, I would include these items:

1. **An Act of the Will.** Dr. Richard Dobbins said, "Never allow yourself to say you can't forgive; be honest and say I won't forgive. You can if you will. It is a choice."

2. **Connected to My Being Forgiven.** The Bible says we are to "Forgive others as we have been forgiven." If we refuse to forgive, something is flawed in our own forgiveness. Only as we go back to the altar to re-experience the depth of our forgiveness do we receive the capacity to forgive.

3. **An Act and a Process.** I worry about fast forgivers. We keep learning the process of forgiveness. In time, levels of forgiveness unfold until, with time, it goes to the depths of our souls.

4. **An Act that Releases You from the Offense.** According to Lewis B. Smedes, "Forgiving is a remedy for pain; but not someone else's pain; just our own." Without forgiveness, it really is like drinking poison and waiting for the other person to die.

5. **An Action that Replaces the Past with the Future.** Let it go. Life is too short. If we don't, it contaminates everything.

Until I read Laura Hillenbrand's book *Unbroken: A World War II Story of Survival, Resilience, and Redemption*, I had never heard of Louis Zamperini.[8] Now I don't think I will ever forget him. Zamperini was born in Olean, New York, on January 26, 1917. After he and his family moved to Torrence, California, he got into a lot of trouble as a teenager. It was then that his brother, Pete, realized Louis could run. Louis qualified for the 1936 Olympic team and was about to break the four-minute mile.

Because the war had started, he enlisted in 1941 and became a pilot of a B-24. On a mission over the Pacific Ocean, mechanical problems forced him to land in the ocean where he was adrift for forty-seven days. Finally, he arrived at land only to be captured by the Japanese.

For three years he faced incredible horror. His nemesis was a prison guard who was nicknamed "The Bird." This man did just about everything to break Zamperini, subjecting him to the kind of inhumane treatment no human being should ever have to face.

When the war ended he was released and able to go home. Severe post-traumatic stress disorder gave him nightmares and drove him to alcohol. His life and marriage hit rock bottom. At that dark moment, his wife went to the Los Angeles Billy Graham Crusade. Her life was transformed and after coaxing him and coaxing him, he finally went with her to a service. On his second visit, he said yes to God.

His life also was transformed. He never had another nightmare. Several years later he went back to Japan to the prison where he was tortured. Although "The Bird" would not see him, he had the opportunity to express forgiveness to many of the other prison guards who had severely mistreated him.

If Jesus could do it and if Joseph could do it and if Desmond Tutu could do it and if Louis Zamperini could do it—we can too. We can forgive. We must forgive.

An unforgiving spirit will do more than grow a root of bitterness. It doesn't matter if you as a leader grow in every other area of your life, nothing will destroy you faster than having an unforgiving spirit. How often we need to pray Psalms 51:10 (KJV), "Create in me a clean heart, O God; and renew a right spirit within me."

Jesus grew in favor with men. Every leader must be able to forgive like Jesus or it will be impossible to grown in favor with men.

CONCLUSION

On May 29, 1953, Edmund Hillary, a thirty-three-year-old Auckland, New Zealand, bee farmer, became the first person to climb to the Himalayan summit of Mount Everest. The world will forever remember that day when Hillary and his Sherpa climbing partner, Tenzing Norgay, stood on the roof of the world at 29,028 feet. From there they looked out over Tibet, Nepal, and India.

Hillary's life began far away from any mountain. As he says in his book *High Adventure: the True Story of the First Ascent of Everest*, "I was sixteen before I ever saw a mountain." His only goal at that age was "a chance to see the world."[9]

But something was planted deeply inside of him on a trip a few years later to the South Island of New Zealand with its Southern Alps. There, as a twenty-year-old young man, he had a chance encounter with some authentic mountain climbers and, after hearing them describe their exploits, he said, "I decided there and then to take up mountaineering."

He decided the next day he had to climb something. And so he did. Just outside the lodge where he was staying were mountains. He could hardly sleep that night, anticipating what the next day would hold. Although his climb the next day did not include a record height, in his words he reached "the summit of my first mountain" and called it "the happiest day I had ever spent." And though he returned home the next day, he later claimed, "My new enthusiasm for the mountains went home with me and gave me little rest in the years that followed."

Over the next years he gave himself to his passion and through a series of amazing encounters joined some of the best mountain climbers in the world. And through those relationships and that growing expertise, he found himself on the quest of his life—to climb Mount Everest. Many had tried before but no man had ever set foot on the top of the world.

His story is one of the greatest adventures I've ever read. I felt as though I was on the expedition with him and his partners as they braved the elements and the terrain to reach their destination.

One of the features that stood out to me was the range of emotions they faced. From sheer fear to utter excitement, they pressed on toward their goal. At times I just knew they would have to turn back. As someone said, "The law of gravity is strictly enforced." Without teamwork, they never could have made it. But even with teamwork and the ropes that tied them together, one slip and they could have plunged thousands of feet to their deaths.

But through it all they persevered. In spite of limited oxygen and fierce winds, they persevered. The goal drew them to the top. And though they only stood on the summit for fifteen minutes, those moments represented for them the quest of a lifetime. As that day ended, Hillary could hardly sleep because of "my overtired body and excited brain."

A few weeks later on July 16, 1953, he was knighted as Sir Edmund Hillary. Over the years he climbed ten other mountain peaks. Hillary once said, "It is not the mountain we conquer but ourselves."

One of the great epitaphs for anyone aspiring to the heights would be, "He died climbing." Anyone committed to becoming like Jesus should aspire to grow like that, with that kind of commitment. How could we possibly be satisfied with doing anything less!

CHAPTER 9

WHY DOES GOD ALLOW ME TO GO THROUGH ADVERSITY?

Between stimulus and response there is a space.
In that space is our power to choose our response.
In our response lies our growth and freedom.
Viktor Frankl

Saints become saints by somehow hanging on to the
stubborn conviction that things are not as they appear
and that the unseen world is as solid and trustworthy
as the visible world around them. God deserves trust,
even when it looks like the world is caving in.
Philip Yancey

Pain is God's megaphone. He whispers to us in
our pleasure but he shouts to us in our pain.
C. S. Lewis

W hen Evie and I left college, we were filled with all of the optimism of young people starting out following the call of God. No challenge seemed too great. We expected to quickly climb every mountain and move easily through every valley we encountered. Pastoring a small church in a small town nestled in the Appalachian Mountains along the

Allegheny River about an hour out of Erie, Pennsylvania, seemed like a place where we could grow and thrive.

We were extremely busy as we learned to love those people and grow on our leadership journey. The church started to grow, which gave us more and more to do. Our hearts and lives were full as we experienced all that God had for us.

About a year later God blessed us with Darin, a happy and healthy little boy. We loved being new parents and soon we moved from our third floor apartment into our own place. God was providing for us and we knew that we were in the center of his will.

A year and a half later Evie was pregnant again, this time with twins. We were thrilled. Her pregnancy was challenging, taxing her small frame. To our surprise, Kevin and Keith arrived six weeks early. Both of them were perfectly healthy except that their lungs were not fully developed. Since it was 1971 and we were in a small-town hospital, technology for premature births was not as advanced as it is today.

As you can imagine, our world immediately ground to a halt. All our attention was on these two little boys. The doctors did everything they could for Keith. He was the most fragile and was not as strong as Kevin. Though the lungs of both boys had not fully developed, Keith battled more than Kevin for air. Today, premature babies are given steroids, and with steroids Keith's breathing, more than likely, would have been normal in just a few days. Over the next two days Keith stopped breathing several times but they were able to resuscitate him. But his little body just couldn't fight hard enough and he entered heaven. He was only two days old. I couldn't hold Evie close enough as we navigated this first major crisis in our marriage. Our hearts were broken. When your world seems to collapse like that, you don't even want to bring yourself to ask the questions which are bouncing around your head.

Kevin was stronger but there was still no guarantee he would make it. The doctors wanted to transport him by ambulance to the neonatal intensive care unit of the Pittsburgh Children's Hospital, about two hours away. Of course we wanted them to do everything they could to save him. So we agreed.

We will never forget the committal service for Keith in that little cemetery of our first town. We had come to the town to grow that church; we never expected something like this would happen. On a warm summer day, the first of August of 1971, and with our hearts crushed and broken, we placed his little body in a tiny wooden casket. We watched as they placed our son in his little casket in the ground. We still return and visit the cemetery and as we view the headstone, all of those emotions still return.

Shortly after the service, we followed the ambulance with our little Kevin inside to Pittsburgh. Over the next days Kevin slowly started to gain weight and his breathing got stronger and stronger. In ten days he was stable enough and strong enough to be brought home.

But how do you send out birth announcements to your friends? Our one eye was weeping and the other eye was smiling. We said it like this, "In the Providence of God He blessed us with twin sons, Kevin and Keith. In His Providence He called Keith home. In His Mercy He allowed Kevin to remain with us."

Once Kevin started eating, he never stopped. Today he stands six feet, two inches. But even today we sometimes wonder how similar to him his identical twin brother, Keith, would have been if he had lived.

As young leaders, how do you deal with that kind of loss? We prayed and trusted God to help us and it seemed as though he had let us down. After they were born we prayed that God would bring them both through that early ordeal, but Keith didn't make it. When you are in the middle of experiences like that you actually wonder how you can go on. Sometimes you just want to leave and go someplace else and get away from all of the pain.

Perhaps the most challenging question we have when we encounter adversity is *where is God in the middle of all this?* If God is good and he is also sovereign, why does he allow us to go through such challenging circumstances? Doesn't he want me to be healthy, cared for, and happy? Or, as Philip Yancey's bestselling book title puts it, *Where Is God When It Hurts?*[1]

Yancey's most recent book goes right to the heart of this matter by addressing *The Question That Never Goes Away*, which is "Why would God allow this to happen?"[2]

We tell our students at UVF that within their first five years they will likely face a test so huge that they will be tempted to give up. The storm they face will test them to the very core of who they are. It will shake the very foundations of their faith. It will change how they view God.

For some it might be with their family, like it was for Evie and me. For others it may be limited finances or people problems or something with health. Adversities come in all shapes and sizes. What do you do when you encounter something that doesn't fit in the little box you imagined your life to be?

I wish my college professors had told me that the furnace was normal in the making of pottery. I wish I had been better prepared. But even if they had said it (and they probably did), my idealism and naivety probably would have hindered me from "getting it."

It doesn't mean that your first test will be the only test you will face; it just means that it will be the first time you will be forced to deal with your idealism smashing up against your reality.

When that happens, how important it is that we learn all that we need to learn in the adversity. Going through that first test will change everything. Others tests come. Sometimes there are several going on at the same time. Sometimes they rain on us like a cloudburst, nearly drowning us. Sometimes they come like a category-five hurricane or tornado or even like a tsunami.

But when they do, without a doubt, they will change us. That one certainly changed Evie and me.

Over the years we have faced many other personal storms with our family and those whom we love. And though the first huge adversity provided us with unforgettable lessons, each one since then has only added to those learning experiences.

But what do you do as a leader when the storm comes against the organization where you are serving? It's one thing to face a personal adversity; it is something else to face an adversity where everyone around you is looking to you and the way you steer the rudder. Everyone looks to the leader in times like that to find assurance that the organization will navigate safely through.

Founded in 1939, UVF is now over seventy-five years old. You just don't go through more than seventy-five years without adversity. Many of those storms took place before Evie and I arrived. We've heard of the times when there was not enough food to feed the students. After praying and praying, God miraculously provided in ways that only could have come from him. God was always faithful.

Former employees speak of another time when funds were tight and salaries were suspended for nearly six months. How indebted we all are to those heroes who remained faithful to God in spite of the adversities they faced. The colors from their courage and sacrifice became part of the fabric which today makes up the university tapestry.

Even after moving to the present campus in 1976, life wasn't always easy. With a presidential change in 1982, the university almost closed. Two board of trustee members stepped up in a board meeting and passionately shared how UVF was needed in the Northeast and beyond. Those words from alumni Rev. Philip Bongiorno (class of 1955) and Rev. Samuel DiTrolio (class of 1957) galvanized the board and they made a decision to remain open.

The crisis was not over. But to navigate that season, God led Dr. J. Robert Ashcroft to come and serve as the new president. Dr. Ashcroft was a distinguished Assemblies of God educator who came out of retirement to become president of UVF. During the next years his servant-leadership style helped to keep the college open. He served over two years, and throughout his tenure he refused to take a salary.

We stand on the shoulders of these heroes. Without their leadership, UVF would, more than likely, not even exist today.

Since Evie and I joined UVF in January 1997, we have also faced many challenges. One of the most serious took place in May 2001. All across the campus exciting things were happening. Our new library had been built. Enrollment was growing. The chapel was expanded to nearly twice its original size. Twenty-seven old military buildings had come down. The momentum was palpable.

For about one year, right in the middle of that campus transformation, we were also receiving large monthly sums of money from a most gracious and generous donor. The total amount that we had deposited in our bank was $1.7 million. During the spring of that year we began to make a list of all of the facilities projects we wanted to address as soon as graduation was over. The list was long.

I'll never forget the moment on that Wednesday night in May that I was told that there was a problem with those funds. I could take you to that very place where I was standing. As it turned out, the donor had done nothing wrong, but the funds he had been receiving were illegally acquired by the individual who made the funds available to him. As a result, the monthly funds not only stopped coming to us, but we knew the only right thing to do was to return all of the money—$1.7 million.

Why does God allow me to go through adversity? Whether the hard times come against us personally or against the organization we are leading, these experiences shape us forever. Sometimes these difficulties almost crush us under their weight. They can cause us to ask *why* we are where we are, and when we look over the horizon to places that do not appear as difficult, we are tempted to change our geography instead of our perspective. And where is God in the middle of it all?

I remember another one of those seasons during our pastoral years when someone had placed our name for consideration at another church that, from a distance, didn't seem to have the problems we were facing. Even today Evie and I quote the words she said then, "If we leave to get away from the problems we now have, there will also be problems there because only the names and faces change. That place will have problems just like this place." We knew God was not leading us away.

But the temptation to run is always there—especially when you're young.

God led the children of Israel through tough times and during those times, he taught them lessons that changed them forever. Deuteronomy 8:1–2 declares, "Be careful to follow every command I am giving you today, so that you may live and increase and may enter and possess the land that the Lord promised on oath to your forefathers. Remember how the Lord led you all the way in the desert these forty years."

But why did Israel have to go through the desert for those forty years? We know initially it was because they had disobeyed God. Of course, most storms we face are not the result of our disobedience. However, I've always cultivated the discipline of searching my heart when storms come to make sure that my heart is surrendered to God's will in every area of my life. Because knowing how to get through a storm or even out of one will depend on how we got into it.

Jonah got into his storm because he disobeyed God. The only way out of that storm was for him to repent. The disciples got into a storm on the Sea of Galilee because Jesus told them to get in the boat. The only way out of that storm was for them, by faith, to ride it out.

But once that is settled for each of us, there is still the haunting question, **Why would God allow me to go through the adversity?** For Israel, God gave them a partial revelation why he led them into the desert. Even though they spent forty years in that desert because of disobedience, what was God really trying to do in them during that season?

If we can understand what God was accomplishing in them during the desert season, it will help our perspective when those times come for us.

THE DESERT WILL HUMBLE YOU

Deuteronomy 8:2 states, "Remember how the Lord your God led you all the way in the desert these forty years to humble and test you." For Israel, the desert reminded them of their lack of faith, disobedience, and ungodliness. Every funeral and every baby dedication taught them humility. Every birthday and every new year taught them humility.

According to Exodus 14:8, Israel was "marching out boldly" from Egypt. This means they were marching out *arrogantly*. Their pride had to be dealt with and the desert addressed it like nothing else.

Deserts humble us. It is the mark of the desert. It's the mark of any adversity. How easy it is to become intoxicated with ourselves. We really can think we're the center of the universe. Adversities compel us to look beyond ourselves.

Someone said that humility is such a delicate subject, the minute we think we have it we don't. Bernard of Clairvaux said, "Learn the lesson, if you are to do the work of a prophet, what you need is not a scepter but a hoe."

Deserts drive us to our knees. Deserts crush our self-centered tendencies. Deserts change us. There is a fragrance of spirit in the desert walker. The person who goes through the "valley of the shadow of death" comes out the other side transformed. You can smell it. You can taste it. We cannot exclude the mark of the desert from our words and actions. It will always show.

Israel was out of Egypt but Egypt wasn't out of Israel. God wanted them to learn humility. If they were ever going to move into the Promised Land, he wanted them to learn to be totally dependent on him. He wanted them to affirm Psalms 20:7, "Some trust in chariots and some in horses, but we trust in the name of the LORD our God."

When you first graduate from college with a newly minted degree, how easy it is to assume you know all the answers. But when you are at the graveside of your baby son and your world has collapsed, or you find yourself needing to return $1.7 million, you quickly learn how dependent you are on God. And we learn new lessons about humility as we cry out to God, "Help me." You realize not only do you not have all the answers; you aren't even sure what the questions should be.

As Dr. J. Robert Ashcroft once said, "Nothing of lasting value ever came out of arrogance. The spirit of Jesus is the spirit of humility."

Why does God allow you to go through adversity? As it was with Israel, so it is with you: To humble you!

THE DESERT WILL TEST YOU

Deuteronomy 8:2 says, "Remember how the Lord your God led you all the way in the desert these forty years to humble and test you in order to know what was in your heart, whether or not you would keep his commands."

Israel had faced many tests. Pharaoh and the Egyptians tested them. The Philistines, the Amorites, Hittites, Hivites, and Jebusites tested them.

In Numbers 16 Moses had to deal with a full-scale mutiny when Korah, Dathan, Abiram, and On came against him with the most vicious opposition. And when Moses invited Dathan and Abiram to meet with him to resolve the matter, they refused saying, "We will not come!" and concluded with words that oozed with sarcasm, "Will you gouge out the eyes of these men? No, we will not come." In other words, they said to Moses, "What are you going to do, Moses? Put out our eyes if we don't cooperate?"

But in spite of all the adversities that tested them, there was no test like the desert. For 40 years they faced that test. 480 months. 175,200 sunrises and sunsets.

Leaders regularly are tested in the desert. And the desert will test you like nothing else will test you. Of course there are deserts—and then there are deserts. Some we get in and out quickly. Others go on and on and on. Sometimes leaders face desert moments. Other times, leaders face desert seasons.

Any plant can grow in a greenhouse. The temperature is controlled to fit perfectly with the plant. The water and fertilizer are calibrated to maximum advantage. The conditions are ideal.

But out in the desert, the temperature can be high and low on the same day. There can be water and drought on the same day. You can eat and starve on the same day. And for Israel, their desert season lasted year after year after year. Forty years.

In the classroom, the lessons come first and the tests come later. In life, the tests come first and the lessons come later.

The adversity exposes us to ourselves. The quality of my faith is exposed in the adversity. The quality of my courage is exposed in the desert.

Joni Eareckson Tada never would have predicted the way her life turned out. As a teenager she enjoyed riding horses, hiking, tennis, and swimming. Her future was bright. But all of that changed on July 30, 1967. She was only seventeen years old when she dove into the Chesapeake Bay, misjudging the shallowness of the water. She suffered a fracture between the fourth and fifth cervical levels and became a quadriplegic, paralyzed from the shoulders down without the use of her hands.

Joni wrote of her experiences in her 1976 international best-selling autobiography, *Joni*. There she described her two years of rehabilitation where she experienced anger, depression, suicidal thoughts, and serious doubts about her Christian faith.

Joni's life is an incredible example of the human spirit to emerge against all odds. And though her life received special joy when in 1981 she married Ken Tada, she faced yet another health challenge in 2010 when she was diagnosed with, and eventually emerged successfully from, breast cancer.

In *God's Plan A* Joni said, "When suffering sandblasts us to the core, the true stuff of which we are made is revealed. Suffering lobs a hand-grenade into our self-centeredness, blasting our soul bare, so we can be better bonded to the Savior."[3]

Gold proves itself in the fire and so do we. God knows we need the test to remove the impurities and all that would hinder our leadership potential.

Why does God allow you to go through adversity? As it was with Israel, so it is with you: to test you!

THE DESERT WILL TEACH YOU

Deuteronomy 8:2–3, "Remember how the Lord your God led you all the way in the desert these forty years…to teach you that man does not live on bread alone but on every word that comes from the mouth of the LORD. Your clothes did not wear out and your feet did not swell during these forty years. Know then in your heart that as a man disciplines his son, so the LORD your God disciplines you."

The desert will take you to school. You will learn more in the desert than you will ever learn in a classroom.

Israel learned that God was enough. Period! Israel learned that God provided all they needed. Israel learned that God disciplined his children because he loved them.

Following her nineteen-year-old son's near fatal accident, Sally Jessy Raphael said, "You can learn more in ten days of agony than ten years of contentment."

Speaking of Saint Basil's faith as being ambidextrous, Gregory of Nicea said he had this two-handed faith "because he welcomed pleasures with the right hand and affliction with the left hand."

Leaders are always learning.

Years ago when we lived in Minnesota I heard about a mural that was being presented to a large audience. Everyone was excited to see the artist's handiwork. The time came for the curtains to be opened and as they opened, the people in the audience were horrified at what they saw. There, in the middle of the picture were two adults hovered over a little boy, appearing to strike him—engaged in behavior that appeared to be child abuse.

As the curtains opened further, however, the wider angle revealed the little family was in the middle of a Minnesota blizzard. And what first appeared as child abuse was actually the fervent effort of those loving parents trying to get circulation back in the limbs of their child.

When we face adversity, how easy it is to accuse God of child abuse. It's like the cartoon with Ziggy standing on the top of a mountain looking up to heaven declaring, "In case you haven't noticed, the good guys are getting creamed down here."

I love the words of the old hymn, "O love that will not let me go." Hosea 13:5 says, "I cared for you in the wilderness, in the land of the burning heat."

Perhaps the darkest period of Israel's history was after the fall of Jerusalem. The book of Jeremiah is God's final attempt to save Jerusalem. But though Jeremiah preached to them for over forty years, he was rejected and persecuted by his own people. Stocks, humiliations, prisons, and cisterns were his constant companions. As the weeping prophet, he gave everything he had, crying out to ears that wouldn't listen and to hands that wouldn't perform and to feet that wouldn't turn.

In spite of his noble effort, Jerusalem was crushed. In 605 BC and then again in 597 BC the mighty Babylonians nibbled at them. Finally in 586 BC they gobbled them up. Lamentations is the funeral dirge over the city. It is the book of Jerusalem's epitaph. In those five hymns of mourning over the fall of Jerusalem, you can hear the death wail of Zion.

Jerusalem, the crown jewel of Israel, the religious and political capital of the people of God, was destroyed. In those 154 verses of parallelism, antithesis, repetition, and plays on words and phrases we encounter, literally, the wailing wall of the Bible.

But in the middle of smoldering Jerusalem, we see the real character of Jeremiah. Erupting out of that horrible context comes this incredible perspective of God. Lamentations 3:21–25 declares that God is love; God is faithful; God is good; and though all was gone, God's presence was still with them.

If Jeremiah could look beyond the indescribable loss of Jerusalem and see the unchanging character of God, you and I as leaders can do the same. When we are in the middle of the desert, we learn God is still there with us.

Often when the problems are complex and the adversity is the greatest, God is faithful to whisper into my heart these words, "This is what I have called you to do. Trust me. I will see you through." Sometimes those words come during a challenging meeting or when I'm preaching or wrestling with the university budget. There is nothing like the assurance that he is there by our side guiding us through.

Only after Abraham demonstrated his incredible obedience and faith did God say to him in Genesis 22:12, "Now I know that you fear God, because you have not withheld from me your son, your only son." We lose the drama of that moment because we know the end of the story. Abraham didn't. Nor do we know the end of our leadership stories.

How well I remember the next two days at UVF after I learned about the $1.7 million problem. The first day I went through the motions. I called the people who needed to be called. With our administrative team we aborted the projects we needed to abort. With God's help, we just did what needed to be done.

By the second day, however, I knew I had to settle matters in my heart. It was then that I reviewed what we did know. *Did God lead us to UVF?* Yes! *Is he the one ultimately in charge of the university?* Yes! *Did this take him by surprise?* No! *Was God still on the throne?* Yes! *Were we going to make it?* Yes!

The most important thing we can learn in times of adversity is that God is right there with us in the middle of it.

During these adversities it feels at times as though God is taking his foot and kicking away the crutches I am prone to lean on. And I want to say how unfair it is. Sometimes I can even feel that I don't need to take it anymore. But as the crutches fall away and all I have to lean upon is God, he whispers to me, "Yes, this is right where I want you. Trust me and I will never let you down. I am enough."

Years ago a Peace Corps volunteer traveled to a South American country where she served for many months out in the bush. Because she was going to be far from modern conveniences, she expected the worst. To her surprise, her hosts had rigged up a makeshift private shower with a water hose which ran cold water into an old can with holes punched in the bottom. She reported how that wonderful gesture made her entire trip.

At the end of her service, she decided to spend her final weekend in that country in a fancy hotel where she would treat herself to some of the modern conveniences she had been without. On the night before she arrived, the hot water heater for the entire hotel broke down and they could not repair it until Monday, the day she was to leave. She said it ruined her entire weekend.

Why does God allow you to go through adversity? As it was with Israel so it is with you: to teach you!

THE DESERT WILL BLESS YOU

Deuteronomy 8:16, "He gave you manna to eat in the wilderness, something your ancestors had never known, to humble and test you so that in the end it might go well with you."

For Israel, God led them through the desert to humble them, to test them, and to teach them. But ultimately, in the end, he wanted everything to go well with them. In spite of all they faced, God had their best interest in mind. He wanted things to go well with them.

Arden Adamson said, "God loves us too much to needlessly allow pain in our lives." His ultimate purpose is to help us become all that he wants us to become and, in the end, to bless us.

When Evie and I were raising our children and we needed to place boundaries in their lives and expectations upon them to hold them accountable, how often we wanted to just scoop them up and make life easier for them.

One of the great privileges I had as a professor was to have my two sons in my classes. I loved it. But the greatest challenge I had was when it was time to give the test. How I wanted to call them up the night before and give them the answers. Of course I couldn't, but their pain caused me pain. I still recall the look on Kevin's face as he took the Historical Books exam and I could see him struggling for an answer.

God in his wisdom allows adversity in order to bless us in the end. And if we are not yet blessed, then it merely means we are not yet at the end. Steve Estes said, "God permits what he hates to accomplish what he loves."

The story of Joseph cannot be understood without including Genesis 50:20, "You intended to harm me, but God intended it for good to accomplish what is now being done, the saving of many lives." The apostle Paul's word helps every leader in the middle of adversity, "And we know that in all things God works for the good of those who love him" (Rom. 8:28).

Frederick Buechner said, "Even the saddest things can become, once we have made peace with them, a source of wisdom and strength for the journey that still lies ahead."

My love for gardening must have had its origins in my early life growing up on a farm where we grew petunias and marigolds. Some years ago I moved from those annuals to perennials. I learned that you plant tulip and allium and daffodil bulbs in the fall before the ground is frozen. The cold of the winter contributes to their growth so when spring comes and the temperature warms up, those bulbs come to life. In the dead of winter I often looked out our kitchen window on the tundra where temperatures would dip to minus twenty and minus thirty degrees with wind chills at times down to minus seventy-five and minus one hundred degrees and think, "Only a gardener knows that there is life under that frozen tundra."

To illustrate how those bulbs need the freezing environment to break open their hard shells, I often bring some along to show as a demonstration. Once, I did that and placed them in a small plastic bag, and when I got home, I put them on a shelf in my closet. Somehow, they got nudged back out of sight and I didn't find them until several months later. To my surprise and dismay, they were soft and mushy like a spoiled onion. They needed the cold and frost and ice and snow to help them.

Now, if I were growing flowers the way I thought they should be grown, I wouldn't do that to them. But when the winter seasons come, we can take great hope that there is life where there does not appear to be life, and that there will be a process which God uses to produce beauty and, though the process is mysterious, he knows what he is doing.

In 1991 Jerry Sittser was traveling with his family on a lonely stretch of highway in rural Idaho. With him were his wife (Lynda), his four children (eight-year-old Catherine, seven-year-old David, four-year-old Diana Jane, two-year-old John) and his mother. Ahead of them a car came swerving into their lane and hit them head on. In his words, "Three generations—gone in an instant"—Lynda, Diana Jane, and his mother.

Once I started reading his compelling book *A Grace Disguised: How the Soul Grows Through Loss,* I could hardly put it down.[4] How could anyone go through such a horrible experience?

Listen to his words, "Catastrophic loss wreaks destruction like a massive flood. It is unrelenting, unforgiving, and uncontrollable, brutally erosive to body, mind and spirit. Sometimes loss does its damage instantly—sometimes loss does its damage gradually. In either case, catastrophic loss leaves the landscape of one's life forever changed."

In the initial shock, Sittser spoke of "unspeakable agony" and being "dizzy with grief's vertigo," pacing the floor "like a caged animal only recently captured." He says, "In one moment my family as I had known and cherished was obliterated."

I had to keep reading, "That initial deluge of loss slowly gave way over the next months to the steady seepage of pain that comes when grief, like floodwaters refusing to subside, finds every crack and crevice of the human spirit to enter and erode. I thought I was going to lose my mind. I was overwhelmed."

With raw transparency Sittser wrote, "The foundation of my life was close to closing in—the loss brought about by the accident had changed my life, setting me on a course down which I had to journey whether I wanted to or not. I was assigned both a tremendous burden and terrible challenge. I faced the test of my life."

We all know, of course, there are many types of loss. Sometimes death is not the most challenging. When my father died and left my mother as a single parent of four children at sixteen, fifteen, twelve, and nine years of age, she later said that her loss was less painful than going through a divorce. At least she had good memories.

Two final comments capture Sittser's thoughts about the accident and his life. "Life will end up being far worse than it would have otherwise been; it will also end up being far better. I will have to endure the bad I do not deserve; I will also get the good I do not deserve."

And finally, "The accident remains now, as it always has been, a horrible experience that did great damage to us and to so many others. It was and will remain a very bad chapter. But the whole of my life is becoming what appears to be a very good book." His final chapter is titled "Life Has the Final Word." And I would add that it is God who has the ultimate word.

Why does God allow you to go through adversity? As it was with Israel, so it is with you: To do you good in the end.

CONCLUSION

The son of a friend of mine smashed his finger, broke the bone in the tip and tore off the whole nail. His father hated to see him in such pain but had to laugh when his son said, "I'm only six—why, God, why?"

When you live as long as I have, you encounter many adversities. Some of them I've mentioned in this chapter. I couldn't begin to list them all here. I've heard it said that if the right subject is brought up, any one of us could be brought to tears in a matter of a few minutes. And sooner or later we wonder why God has allowed that in our lives.

But how we respond to those adversities changes everything. The same sun that melts butter hardens clay. If we face them and we get angry and hard and bitter, we will allow the desert experiences to ruin us. But if we allow them to crush the self part of us, the part that is not like God, those things will transform us into the image of God. But it is our choice.

Viktor Frankl was a Holocaust survivor who wrote a book about his experience titled *Man's Search for Meaning*. He made a strong case for personal responsibility when we face any adversity, even something as horrific as the Holocaust. He said, "Between stimulus and response there is a space. In that space is our power to choose our response. In our response lies our growth and freedom."[5] We all have a choice how we respond in that space.

And it is in that space that life rises and falls when we are in the desert.

Tsang Tsz-Kwan is an amazing twenty-year-old young woman from Hong Kong, China. If you were to pass her on the sidewalk, she would look like an average student in Hong Kong with her standard-issue blue shift dress with a Chinese collar and practical black shoes.

Tsang's determination helped her in a recent test to score within the top 5 percent in nearly all her subjects in the city's college entrance examinations. You may wonder what could be so amazing about her and her accomplishments.

Tsang has been blind and severely hearing impaired from a young age. She also has weak sensitivity in her fingertips, which prevents her from being able to feel the raised dots of Braille characters. But rather than give up, she found a different way to read Braille—with her lips.

She refused to allow her adversity to define her. Between stimulus and her response there was a space and she did something incredible in that space. Next time I'm tempted to complain about the less-than-perfect circumstances that are upon me, I will remember the blind and nearly deaf Chinese young woman who reads Braille with her lips.

Often, when the tempest rages and I don't know the answer, I think about that space. In that space between stimulus and response I also can choose how to respond. And the response I keep coming back to is asking the question, *What can I learn from this adversity? What is God trying to teach me?*

Charles Spurgeon answered the question like this, "Many people owe the grandeur of their lives to their tremendous difficulties. The Lord gets his best soldiers out of the highlands of affliction." God does not throw us into deep water to drown us but to clean us up and to teach us how to swim. Sure, like the disciples we may find ourselves "straining at the oars" (Mark 6:48), but we know that God is doing deep things in us to teach us to trust him.

Of course, all we do is for the glory of God. And according to Isaiah 42:8, "I am the LORD; that is my name! I will not give my glory to another or my praise to idols." No one is immune to the storms of life. The followers of Jesus should be able to take a punch better than anyone else. And when we survive the storm and are still standing after we are beaten up by the adversity, the fact that we have survived brings ultimate glory to God.

We would ask one more time, **Why does God allow me to go through adversity?**

This would be Thomas Merton's reply:

> *Souls are like wax waiting for a seal.... The wax that has melted in God's will can easily receive the stamp of its identity, the truth of what it was meant to be. But the wax that is hard and dry and brittle and without love will not take the seal: for the hard seal, descending upon it, grinds it to powder.*
>
> *Therefore if you spend your life trying to escape from the heat of the fire that is meant to soften and prepare you to become your true self, and if you try to keep your substance from melting in the fire—as if your true identity were to be hard wax—the seal will fall upon you at last and crush you. You will not be able to take your true name and countenance, and you will be destroyed by the event which was meant to be your fulfillment.*[6]

When these times come, and they will, may we always be "prisoners of hope" (Zech. 9:12).

PART III

THE LEGACY
QUESTION

CHAPTER 10

How Do I Want to Be Remembered on Earth and Received in Heaven?

Your story is the greatest legacy you leave to your friends.
It's the longest-lasting legacy you will leave to your heirs.
Steve Saint

We must begin thinking like a river if we are to leave
a legacy of beauty and life for future generations.
David Brow

I have fought the good fight, I have finished the race,
I have kept the faith. Now there is in store for me the
crown of righteousness, which the Lord, the righteous
Judge, will award to me on that day—and not only to
me, but also to all who have longed for his appearing.
Paul, the Apostle (2 Tim. 4:7–8)

No matter how old you are, sooner or later the legacy question will come up. And the earlier you begin asking it, the more likely it is that you'll give answers you can live with and die with. Certainly, our legacy will be framed by how we keep answering all of the questions we have been asking throughout this book as well as how we have been living the answers. How we answer each one will contribute something to how we will be remembered on earth and how we will be received in heaven.

Let's review them:

The Lofty Question
1. *What Does It Mean to Be a Follower of Jesus?*

The Life Questions
2. *What Is the Culture of the Organization?*
3. *What Is Expected of Me?*
4. *How Do I Lead with Vision?*
5. *What Does It Mean to Follow/Lead and to Lead/Follow?*
6. *How Do I Effectively Manage My Time?*
7. *How Do I Balance My Public Life and My Private Life?*
8. *How Do I Keep Growing as a Leader?*
9. *Why Does God Allow Me to Go Through Adversity?*

The Legacy Question
10. *How Do I Want to Be Remembered on Earth and Received in Heaven?*

The older I get the more funerals I attend. And with each one we are relentlessly reminded that, sooner or later, people will be attending ours. We know the statistics—no one gets out of this life alive.

We all prepare for funerals differently. Even if the service is close by, we must change our schedules if we are to attend. The daily routines are set aside, even if only for a few hours.

From the clothes we wear to the cards we send and from the words we say to the flowers we give, each of us tries to express love and care and sympathy in different verbal and non-verbal ways.

For those of us who are clergy, we know that a funeral is unlike any other ministerial responsibility. The event is laden with enormous variety and emotion. A funeral for a child is very different than a funeral for someone who just celebrated her one-hundredth birthday. Death caused by a prolonged illness is very different from the home-going of a loved one who died suddenly or unexpectedly. Some people who die leave behind countless family and friends while others seemingly lived rather solitary lives.

As a teenager I attended my father's funeral, and as a twenty-four-year-old father I attended my son's funeral. My mother died when I was forty-four years old. We can be confronted with legacy issues at just about any age.

Before the start of a recent funeral service, Evie and I sat with the other mourners looking at the pictures on the screen of our dear friend. We always find those moments deeply moving. Baby pictures. Parents. Siblings. Friends. Neighbors. Spouse. Children. Hobbies. Colleagues. Vacations. Travel. Happy days. A life well lived.

At those moments the issue of legacy inevitably fills the room. How long did the person live? Who was influenced by his life? What did she leave behind that matters in light of eternity? If he lived his life over again, what would he have done differently? If she were in her own funeral service, would she have any regrets?

Funerals cause us to think about our own legacy. We ask ourselves those questions. On the day of my funeral, what will be the legacy I leave behind? In light of what really matters, will my life really have mattered?

Often when I am asked to share a few words at a funeral I find myself quoting Henry Wadsworth Longfellow's legacy statement, "Great men (and women) stand like solitary towers in the City of God." Or I will quote the poet Rabindranath Tagor who said, "Death is not extinguishing the light. It is turning out the lamp because the dawn has come."

When Evie and I first came to UVF we were warmly welcomed by a host of wonderful new friends. Among them were John and Esther Hammercheck. We will never forget when they invited us to go cherry picking in Lancaster County, Pennsylvania. One of the favorite pictures I have ever taken is of John with his dapper hat among some cherry-laden branches on that beautiful summer day. Nor will we forget those times they hosted us with other friends to that fancy New Jersey restaurant where we feasted on an all-you-can-eat lobster buffet. I still remember his incredible sense of humor and the way he made us laugh when he preached or just visited with us one-on-one. What dear friends they were indeed!

All of us who attended their funerals, which were several years apart, mutually shared emotions of joy and sadness; joy because we knew them and sadness because of our sorrow that they were gone. We loved sharing stories about them and, even though they did not have any children, their influence was almost legendary.

Sometime later there arrived at my desk a legacy gift from the Hammerchecks. I remember looking at their generous gift and remembering all of the wonderful times we had had together. It was a sacred moment. I hardly wanted to hold the check, much less cash it, because this represented their very lives. But of course we did, to honor their deep desire to help make their alma mater a better place for the next generation of leaders. I always feel that way when similar gifts come to UVF.

Years ago I was visiting with a funeral director about what goes through the mind of a funeral director when he's not on the job. I mentioned that farmers notice fields and barns and cattle and machinery. I mentioned that ministers notice churches and books and human behaviors.

"What about you?" I asked. I will never forget his answer. "Let me put it this way," he said. "I don't walk through cemeteries on my days off."

And though that comment still makes me smile, I do know some people enjoy walking through cemeteries to read the epitaphs on the tombstones. Most of the time epitaphs are serious summaries of a person's earthly journey. For Evie's mother we chose these two simple words, "Finally home."

But some epitaphs make us smile. A cemetery in Silver City, Nevada, has these words on the tombstone, "Here lies a man named Zeke. Second fastest draw in Cripple Creek."

In Waynesville, North Carolina, Effie Jean Robinson's epitaph (1897–1922), "Come blooming youths, as you pass by; and on these lines do cast an eye. As you are now, so once was I; As I am now, so must you be; Prepare for death and follow me."

THE DISTINGUISHING MARK OF LEADERSHIP

Those words are not funny but underneath someone added, "To follow you I am not content; How do I know which way you went."

In high school I was given an assignment to write my own epitaph. I have long forgotten what I wrote but if I wrote it today, I wonder what I would say. What would you say if you wrote yours?

How will I be remembered on earth? Here are some micro-questions that, if answered appropriately, will help how I answer that question.

How do small things contribute to my legacy? How easy it is to be enamored with big things. Unless it makes headlines and wins prizes and captures the attention of the masses, some of us don't want to be bothered with small things. How important is my cup of water in a world filled with a limitless supply of bottled water? How does my widow's mite matter in a world of gigantic resources? The prophet Zechariah said, "Who despises the day of small things?"

The smallest gesture has the potential to leave the largest legacy. If God used the ox goad of Shamgar, the sling of David, the jawbone of a donkey with Samson, the perfume of Mary, the rod of Aaron, the needle of Dorcas, and the five loaves and two fish of the little boy to leave legacies, what can he do with the little bit that you have?

As I look back on the legacies I have received from others, their influence in my life may have been small at the time, but the ongoing echoes of that gesture have stayed with me to this day. A brief word of encouragement and small nod of approval can breathe life into us.

After my father died and my mother became a single parent of four, she would often say the same thing when something went wrong on the farm. It almost became a kind of mantra. If a piece of machinery would break down or it would rain on the crop about to be harvested or if we had a problem with an animal, she would say, "It's just at the barn." To us, her family, we knew exactly what she meant: it was not a problem with one of us. It was not a problem with a family member; it really was "just at the barn."

Over the years Evie and I have found ourselves repeating that simple sentence to remind ourselves of what really matters in life. My mother's legacy lives on and on through us.

Even a small gift can make a large difference. Evie and I will never forget the time we lacked the remaining $25 to pay the first month's rent of our first apartment at our first pastorate in Franklin, Pennsylvania. It was due on July 1, 1968. On that very day we received a note from a former college classmate who said he had been praying for us and sensed a nudge from God to send us some money. In the envelope was a check for $25. After we cashed it and paid our rent, we were just as poor as before, but today the legacy of that gift remains with us. God divinely provided our rent money!

If I plant something today, will it bear fruit tomorrow? We will probably never know the full effect of our legacy. But just because we don't know all that it may mean tomorrow doesn't mean we should minimize our efforts today.

One of the most remarkable examples of the power of a seed is the date palm that sprouted in 2005 from a seed recovered from Masada, near the Dead Sea in Israel. It is the oldest seed known to have sprouted and is estimated to be about two thousand years old.

If God can do that with an old seed, what do you think he can do with the legacy seeds you plant today? The law of sowing and reaping will inevitably produce life and fruit to what you plant. So, keep planting and planting and planting.

Some years after Evie and I were married we were visiting my mother on the farm where she lived just outside of Lebanon, Pennsylvania. I happened to look out the window and I saw her walk across the lawn on that narrow limestone sidewalk until she came to the edge of the small country road. She paused, crossed the road, and reached into her mailbox to get the mail.

That image had a huge effect on me. I realized she did that every day. I make a decision right then to send her a postcard each Monday morning from wherever I was. Over the years I kept up that habit. I gathered postcards from small towns in the upper Midwest and in places overseas where I traveled. I always bought two cards: one for me and one for her.

When she died, our family was going through her personal things in that little farmhouse and there in the second drawer of her dresser was a box with all the postcards I had ever sent her. My only regret that day was that I hadn't sent her more. We never know how our small gestures will impact those whom we love.

How can I make sure that my legacy will matter even now? When Evie and I were celebrating our fortieth wedding anniversary, I wanted to give her something she would remember. I found a software program on the Internet called Blurb, which can be downloaded to make a book using digital pictures.

The result was a compilation of photographs that captured the places we lived and the people who mattered to us. We still look at it and smile.

After doing that, we decided to do the same for our grandson, Noah. Since he lives in Minnesota, we get to see him about five times a year. During those treasured times, I take lots of pictures, which go into the book we give him as a birthday gift in February each year. We've been doing this for a number of years and each book captures all we did that year. He calls me Poppy and now says, "Here Poppy, take this picture—for my book." But as we think of our family legacy for him and our children and our relatives, we want it to extend far beyond just a book.

My life has been shaped by the legacy of my maternal grandmother. I am one of twenty-six grandchildren, and when each of us got married, she gave us a subscription to *Guideposts* magazine. My whole life was transformed by the writings of some of the key authors in that little magazine. Even today, though my grandmother entered heaven many years ago and now we subscribe to *Guideposts,* I still think of her when it comes each month as well as the legacy she left me. I also still have the crib quilt she made as a gift for each of her grandchildren, including me.

My mother left us with an enormous legacy too countless to try to itemize here. Her quiet and gentle and godly spirit influences me to this day.

As I look back at those memories and the memories of countless family members, friends, colleagues, and mentors over the years, I keep asking, *What legacy am I leaving even now on those around me?*

I still remember driving back to college across Illinois and looking over at Evie, my new bride, and realizing that the way I live in front of her from then on could, more than likely, affect her eternal destiny.

Bernard Loiseau was a very famous man. His skill and personality catapulted him into the rare world of French cuisine. He ran one of only twenty-five restaurants in France awarded three stars by the all-powerful Michelin. Throughout his career, his restaurant in Saulieu in Burgundy had been ranked by another restaurant guide, GaultMillau, 19 out of a possible 20 points.

"We are selling dreams; we are merchants of happiness," he once said. With no formal schooling or gourmet pedigree, Loiseau was passionate about his work. Throughout France he was known as "Monsieur 100,000 Volts" who had received France's Legion of Honor in 1995.

Then, for the first time ever, his GaultMillau rankings dipped from 19 points to 17 points and there were rumors (which never materialized) that his Michelin rating would drop to 2 stars. So, after serving lunch in early March 2003, Loiseau went to his bedroom for his customary nap and, at age fifty-two, committed suicide. Loiseau once told a fellow chef that if he lost a star, life would not be worth living.

How sad that the legacy he left during his lifetime rose and fell with a restaurant rating scale. How sad that he framed the value of his whole life on that kind of review. How much did his obsession really matter even in this life?

Will my legacy be important in light of eternity? On a shelf in my office, just below a painting of the family farm where I grew up, is my father's Bible. After he died my mother received it and after she died, it came to me. I usually have it open to one of his (and her) favorite verses in Luke 12:15, "Life does not consist in the abundance of possessions."

Some people have an unusual attachment with things. One businessman said, "If you think making money is hard, try giving it away." If we don't have a giver's heart, causing us to hold things with an open hand, it's unlikely that we will leave a legacy that will be important in light of eternity. As Erich Fromm said, "Greed is a bottomless pit which exhausts the person in an endless effort to satisfy the need without ever reaching satisfaction." One wealthy man was asked how much he needed to satisfy himself and he replied, "Just a little bit more."

In 1886 Leo Tolstoy wrote a short story with a timeless message about a man who, in his lust for land, forfeited everything. In his "How Much Land Does a Man Need?" a peasant named Pahom complained that he didn't have enough land to satisfy him. He claimed, "If I have plenty of land, I shouldn't fear the Devil himself."

The story describes his insatiable quest to get more land. He arrives in a land where he made a deal with the leader. For an agreed amount, he could purchase all of the land he could walk around completely between sun up and sun down. The tragic ending graphically describes how his greed caused him to run and run to try to get back to the place he started in time. But as the sun was setting, he collapsed at that place and died.

To the question, *How much land does a man need?* Tolstoy illustrated tragically and ironically, he only really needed enough for his grave.

Nothing is quite as sobering as walking through an empty house where family members once lived. For fourteen years Warren and Mildred Morneau lived at the house on 3107 Elim Avenue in Zion, Illinois.

The atmosphere changed dramatically when her mother, Mildred, died. And seventeen months later, after an extended illness and complications from diabetes and two surgeries, Warren died on January 20, 2004.

Personal reflection comes easily when a close family member dies. Conversations in hotel restaurants and funeral receiving lines recapture echoes from over the years. Old wrinkled black-and-white photographs resurrect a million memories.

A few days before the funeral, Evie and her sister, Margie, closed up the house. With care, personal items were distributed to family and friends. The rest was sold and within a few short hours a house that once bustled with veterans of the Great Depression stood empty.

On the day of the funeral Evie and I walked through the house one more time, holding hands together. How strange it felt as we took the key from the mailbox and opened the front door. No one was there to greet us. Somehow we felt like we were violating her parents' personal space. The smell of fried chicken and the taste of that "world-famous" potato salad were not to be found. The loud television for their faltering hearing was not to be heard. The house was empty.

Slowly we walked from room to room. We saw the curtains Evie picked out with her mother. In the kitchen was the old refrigerator and gas stove. The washer and drier were resting like lonely sentinels against a cement block wall. The *Sorry* game was not in the closet.

Yes, the house was empty. No pictures. No furniture. No knickknacks. No knives for me to sharpen. No microwave. No toaster. No clothing. No books. No sounds. Nothing. It was all gone. Even the old wooden sign "Welcome: The Morneau's—Warren and Millie" was gone from the front porch.

I remembered a sermon years ago preached by my friend Dr. Don Argue, whose father had died after spending his final years in a nursing home. All his earthly possessions from his entire life were placed in two cardboard boxes. To illustrate our mortality in his sermon, Don placed two cardboard boxes on the table in front of the congregation. I don't think any of us will ever forget the sight of those two boxes.

That empty house in Zion, Illinois, was the end of an era. Two daughters are without parents; two sons-in-law without in-laws; four grandchildren without grandparents; and two great-grandsons and one great-granddaughter are without great-grandparents.

For the last time we walked out the front door. For the first time there was no one to hear us say goodbye. For the last time we closed the door. The key was placed back in the mailbox. As we backed out of the driveway, only in our memories did we see two people standing at the open door waving goodbye. The house was really empty. But Warren and Millie Morneau were not in the house. The legacy of their lives was left in all who knew them.

I also know there will be a day when I leave my office for the very last time. The calendar always wins. When that day comes, I will take my books off the shelves. The pictures will come off the walls. I will pack up in boxes every artifact I have gathered or have been given. I will chair my last meeting. I will lead my last UVF chapel service. Until then, this question keeps informing every part of my private and public life.

But I also think Elizabeth Kubler-Ross understood something important when she said, "Live so you do not have to look back and say, 'God, how I wasted my life.'" This sounds like the tragic description of Jehoram, a man who was thirty-two years old when he became king, and he reigned over Jerusalem for eight years. In 2 Chronicles 21:20 we read these sad words, "He passed away, to no one's regret."

At the beginning of my personal mission statement I have placed these words from Joshua 22:3, "You...have completed the mission the Lord your God gave you." If I wanted to summarize my life's goal it would be in the two simple words, "mission accomplished."

In mid-career, the Russian short-story writer Isaac Babel was hustled away, but Babel was heard to shout, "But I was not given time to finish!" I suppose most of us will always feel that way. When the end of our life comes, most of us will want to have just a little more time.

But, no matter how much time we have been given by God, may we all say with the apostle Paul, "For I am already being poured out like a drink offering, and the time for my departure is near. I have fought the good fight, I have finished the race, I have kept the faith" (2 Tim. 4:6–7).

Which brings us to the second part of this question:

How will I be received in heaven? 2 Timothy 4:8 continues, "Now there is in store for me the crown of righteousness, which the Lord, the righteous Judge, will award to me on that day—and not only to me, but also to all who have longed for his appearing."

On our old farmhouse wall where I grew up I remember seeing countless times a faded plaque that said it all, "Only that is important which is eternal." One day each of us will stand before God and give an account of how we lived our lives.

Revelation 20:11–12 speaks of that day, "Then I saw a great white throne and him who was seated on it. The earth and the heavens fled from his presence, and there was no place for them. And I saw the dead, great and small, standing before the throne and books were opened."

When I read those words I realize again the importance of the question, *How will I be received in heaven?* I have a friend who, when asked what is his deepest desire, he always replies, "to have the favor of God."

Many years ago a story from England told of a criminal named Charles Peace. He was a burglar, and he was guilty of double murder. He was condemned to death for his crimes. As he was making his way to the gallows on the day of his execution, a chaplain walked by his side. This minister was simply "going through the motions," speaking coldly of the importance of faith and belief. In the course of his oft-repeated speech, the minister mentioned the power of Jesus Christ to save from sin.

Suddenly the criminal spun around, looked the chaplain in the eye and exclaimed, "Do you believe that? Do you really believe that? If I believed that, I would willingly crawl across England on broken glass to tell men it was true."

Imagine that day when you stand before God. That day anticipated by the prophets of old, the great day of the Lord.

On that day, every wrong will be made right. All tears will be wiped away. There will be no night.

In the words of the old gospel song:[1]

It will be worth it all
When we see Jesus
Life's trial will seem so small
When we see Him.
One glimpse of His dear face
All sorrows will erase
So bravely run the race
'Till we see Christ.

CONCLUSION

CONCLUSION

*This is where people learn the questions
that require a lifetime to answer.*
Advertisement for the William Mitchel College of Law

*I refuse to answer that question on the
grounds that I don't know the answer.*
Douglas Adams

The important thing is not to stop questioning.
Albert Einstein

I n *Leading with Soul*, Lee Bolman and Terrence Deal say, "The responsibility of the guide is not to give answers, but to raise questions, suggest directions to explore, and to offer support."[1] Throughout this book I have tried to do just that.

I trust you understand more clearly why I suggest that the distinguishing mark of leadership is the question mark. The questions we keep asking do indeed function as those pieces of glass between the sections of the pillars of the old cathedral in Nantwich, England. Those telltales really do tell the tale of the foundation and architecture of the structure.

In the same way, our questions challenge our thoughts and our motives and our leadership and, ultimately, our life. And we must keep asking them and answering them because we keep changing and everything around us keeps changing. Socrates used this method. Jesus used this method. You and I can and must use this method as well.

I suggest you make your own list of questions. These questions are merely a sample of leadership questions I have asked on my leadership journey. But they are definitely not comprehensive. I trust that these questions will assist you on your leadership journey in three ways.

First, you may want to use these as a kind of telltale checklist. They are important and to miss these could cause you to miss some of the most critical leadership issues you will face.

Second, you may want to add more questions to the ones that are here. Earlier I called these *micro-questions* because they ask more specific questions about the broader, more comprehensive question. It's always appropriate to come at the broader question from many different directions.

Third, you may want to expand this list to include specific questions that you know you'll want to keep asking. Each of us is unique and each of our lives and leadership situations is different. To learn this mark of leadership will equip you to keep growing in every area of your life. As Nancy Willard said, "Some questions are more important than answers."

One of my favorite stories comes out of the world of music. As the story goes, a Stradivarius violin was going to be played at a special concert in a given town hall. The possibilities of being a part of this historic moment captured the entire community. The media picked up the story. Articles were published about this exquisite instrument: the wood, the strings, the varnish, the many Antonio Stradivarius made, how many were left in the world, etc. The radio and television did their part to communicate this once-in-a-lifetime experience.

In all of the excitement, not one word was mentioned about the man who was going to play this instrument at the concert. This huge omission frustrated him beyond measure. He had to do something about it. Without telling anyone, he went out the night before the concert and bought a very cheap violin, what we would call a dime-store violin.

The night of the concert arrived. The hall was packed. The curtains opened as a hush filled the room. The violinist played his first song on the dime-store violin. The music was indescribable. When he finished, the applause was deafening.

As soon as everything quieted down and he was to begin his second song, he took that violin by the neck and walked over to an empty piano bench, and, with all of the frustration that had been building in him for weeks, he smashed it to bits. Everyone gasped with horror.

He then walked to the middle of the stage holding up what was left of the violin and at the top of his voice he cried out, "It's not the violin, it's the violinist that makes the difference." They then brought the Stradivarius out on a pillow and he played the rest of the concert on the Stradivarius.

Over the years that story has reminded me in the personal and public parts of my life of the delicate balance between my part and God's part in leadership influence. Ultimately we are merely the instruments and God is the Master Violinist. As the apostle Paul says in 2 Corinthian 3:5–6, "Not that we are competent in ourselves to claim anything for ourselves, but our competence comes from God. He has made us competent as ministers of a new covenant."

Our use of the distinguishing question mark on our life's leadership journey will have resulted in God's figurative use of the exclamation point in his "Mission Accomplished" when we will hear his words, "Well done, good and faithful servant." On that day, nothing else will matter.

Bob Benson captures this meaning in his classic poem titled "He Said His Lines"[2]

> One of our sons, Mike,
>   wanted to take private speech.
> He's such a talker anyway,
>   I recommended hush instead.
> But it was inexpensive
>   and he was interested,
>   so we let him.
>
> The climax of the year's labor
>   was a two-hour assortment
>   of clowns, kings, rabbits,
>   and forgotten lines
>   known as the Speech Recital,
>   given to a devoted audience
>   of eager parents
>   and trapped friends.
> Mike was a king.
>   He looked rather regal, too,
>   if I do say so myself.
> At least until the queen,
>   a head taller and

twenty pounds heavier,
stood beside him
casting a pall on his regality.
He had only three lines to say—
nine months of speech,
three short lines.
And they came very late,
in the last moment
of the last act
of the very last play.

Anyway you looked at it
he was not the star,
at least to anyone except
a couple about halfway back
on the left side.

It was a long evening
and it was miserably hot.
But Mike waited
and he was ready
and he said his lines
and he said them well.
Not too soon, not too late,
not too loud, not too soft,
but just right,
he said his lines.

I'm just a bit player, too,
not a star in any way.
But God gave me a line or so
in the pageant of life,
and when the curtain falls

and the drama ends,
and the stage is vacant at last,
I don't ask for a critic's raves
or fame in any amount.
I only hope that He can say,
"He said his lines.
Not too soon, not too late,
not too loud, not too soft,
he said his lines
and he said them well."

ACKNOWLEDGMENTS

One final question remains: *Who are the people who helped you write this book?* Answering that question is extremely important because any writing project like this reflects the influence of countless individuals. And since some of my observations reach back more than five decades, I obviously am unable to include everyone who directly or indirectly helped me. But here are a few of them.

The sources of quotes, illustrations and stories: Anyone who is around me very long soon discovers that I like quotes. Actually, I love them. I've been collecting them for as long as I can remember. When I was in high school I had a large scrapbook where I taped the ones I found to the pages. Since then I've compiled them in an electronic file.

If you were to ask me where I got them I'd have to say just about everywhere. Over the years I found them in the books I read and the conversations I had and the sermons I heard. I found them in magazines and in newspapers and in brochures. I found them on billboards and on the sides of buildings and on the Internet. Sometimes I have intentionally looked for them, and other times they just appeared in the middle of life. I love the ones I found in the magazines in the dentist's office or on an airplane. As I said, I found them everywhere.

Since I have been collecting them all my life, I now have over five thousand. Someday I might also publish them in a book. I am hardly ever without a pen and a index card to write them down or now, a smart phone with a voice memo. As someone said, "The faintest pencil is mightier than the greatest memory."

The ones I have included in this book are, to the best of my ability, as accurate as I could possibly remember or as I wrote them down when I first heard them. Any errors are certainly not intentional.

The people who have indirectly helped me write this book: I would first mention the authors who have influenced me through their writings. Elton Trueblood, Thomas Merton, Philip Yancey, Henri J. M. Nouwen, Dietrich Bonhoeffer, Leonard Sweet, John Piper, Gordon MacDonald, Elizabeth Elliot, Os Guinness, Mark Batterson, Parker J. Palmer, Dallas Willard, Richard Foster, St. John of the Cross, Alan Nelson, Augustine, Norman Vincent Peale, Morten Kelsey, and many more who spoke into my life on what it means to follow Jesus.

John Maxwell, Harvey Mackay, Larry Donnithorne, Henry Blackaby, Warren Bennis, John Kotter, Jim Collins, Malcolm Gladwell, Terrence Deal, Lee Bolman, Stephen Covey, Peter Senge, Mark McCormack, Hudson T. Armerding, Robert E. Quinn, and many more spoke into my life on what it means to be a leader.

I have also been privileged to sit at the feet of some outstanding teachers/professors/mentors who, through their words and their actions, have taught me more than I could ever repay. I keep drawing from the well of information and inspiration with which they have entrusted to me.

The people who have directly helped me: Thank you, Debbie Capeci, for your excellent editorial and publishing assistance. Without you, this project would never have been completed.

Thank you, Dave Whitcomb, for your generous gift which helped make the publishing of this book a reality.

I will always be grateful for Dr. Dan Mortensen, UVF Executive Vice President and Vice President of Development, for asking me to share some thoughts on leadership to a group of student leaders-in-training. Though that request was many years ago, it caused me to ponder what helped me most on my own leadership journey, and that has led me since then to this topic of leadership questions.

I will also always be grateful for Dr. Don Argue. In 1976 while he was the academic dean at North Central University (formerly North Central Bible College), he invited me to join the faculty where I served as a professor for three years. After he became the president of NCU in 1979, he invited me to serve as the academic dean, where I served with him for the sixteen years he was president and then two more years with his successor, Dr. Gordon Anderson. Then in 1996 Dr. Argue recommended me to the UVF search committee to be considered as president where I subsequently began my current ministry on January 1, 1997.

At those three significant seasons in my life, Dr. Argue's influence was strategic. I will always be grateful to him for believing in me on those two occasions to invite me and on one occasion to recommend me to leadership positions for which I had no prior experience. Over the years, his personal friendship and leadership have profoundly affected and continues to affect my life.

The person who has helped me the most: But, without a doubt, the most influential person in my entire life and also with this book is my dear sweetheart and wife, Evie. Ever since August 5, 1967, when I had the privilege of changing her last name, we have walked arm-in-arm and heart-to-heart on our personal and leadership journey. Her help with this book as an editor has been incalculable. But she is far more than a masterful wordsmith. As I wrestled with what to include and what to omit and how to say it and how not to say it, her help was priceless.

She has been my greatest encourager. The joy of my life began when she and I became "we." To tell her "thank you" could never capture all that is in my heart.

I would also mention the encouragement that has come over the years from our two sons, Darin and Kevin, and of course Noah, the most awesome grandson in the world. Having them in our family plants an unending quest in me to be a better father, grandfather, and leader.

My thanks to God: My expressions of appreciation certainly include the many people (mentioned and unmentioned) who have helped me write this book. But I also want to express my gratitude to God for his faithfulness over the years on my leadership journey. Years ago a mentor said, "Be careful what you think of God because it impacts all of your life." I would agree.

God has led Evie and me on this leadership journey and any insights of worth which I have included here have come because of those which I have received from him. To God be the glory!

NOTES

INTRODUCTION

1. Robert Henri, *The Art Spirit* (New York: Harper & Row Publishers, 1923), 120; 175.

2. Stephen R. Covey, *The 7 Habits of Highly Effective People* (New York: Simon & Schuster, 1989), 95.

CHAPTER 1

1. Dietrich Bonhoeffer, *The Cost of Discipleship* (New York: Collier Books, 1937, 1959, 1960, 1961, 1963PB), 7.

2. Leonard Sweet and Frank Viola, *Jesus Manifesto* (Nashville: Thomas Nelson, 2010), 161ff.

3. Mrs. Howard Taylor, *Borden of Yale '09: The Life That Corrects* (China Inland Mission, 1913).

4. Alan E. Nelson, *Broken in the Right Place: How God Tames the Soul* (Nashville: Thomas Nelson Inc, 1994), 1ff.

5. C. S. Lewis, *Mere Christianity* (New York: HarperCollins, 1952).

6. Os Guinness, *Prophetic Untimeliness* (Grand Rapids: Baker Books, 2003), 11.

CHAPTER 2

1. Peter M. Senge, *The Fifth Discipline: The Art and Practice of the Learning Organization* (New York: Doubleday Currency, 1990).

2. Victor Hugo, trans. By Norman Denny, *Les Miserables* (New York: Penguin Classics, 1862, 1982), 491.

3. James C. Collins and Jerry I. Porras, *Built to Last: Successful Habits of Visionary Companies* (New York: Harper Business, 1994), Chapter 6, 115ff.

4. Mark H. McCormack, *What They Don't Teach You at the Harvard Business School* (Toronto: Bantam Books, 1984).

5. Jim Collins, *Good to Great* (New York: Harper Business, 2001), 1.

CHAPTER 3

1. Susan Resneck Pierce, *On Being Presidential: A Guide for College and University Leaders* (San Francisco: Jossey-Bass, 2012), xi.

2. Hudson T. Armerding, *Leadership* (Wheaton: Tyndale House Publishers, Inc, 1978).

3. Robert E. Quinn, *Deep Change: Discovering the Leader Within* (San Francisco: Jossey-Bass, 1996).

4. Mac Anderson and Tom Feltenstein, *Change Is Good... You Go First* (Naperville: Simple Truths, 2007).

5. Norman Vincent Peale, *The Power of Positive Thinking* (New York: Prentice-Hall, 1952).

6. Jim Collins, *Good to Great* (New York: Harper Collins Publishers, Inc, 2001), Chapter 1, 1ff.

CHAPTER 4

1. George W. Cornell, "At 81, Mother Teresa's Mission Remains Unchanged," for Associated Press, 1992.

2. A. N. Wilson, *Tolstoy* (New York: W. W. Norton & Company, 1988), ix.

3. Henri, *The Art Spirit*, 66.

4. Dr. & Mrs. Howard Taylor, *Hudson Taylor's Spiritual Secret* (Chicago: Moody Press, 1935).

5. David Wilkerson, *The Cross and the Switchblade* (New York: Jove Books, 1962, 1977).

6. Robert Fulghum, *Maybe (Maybe Not): Second Thoughts from a Secret Life* (New York: Villard Books, 1993).

7. Frank Schaeffer, *Addicted to Mediocrity* (Westchester: Cornerstone Books, 1981).

8. Ralph Waldo Emerson, "The Divinity School Address" to the Senior Class at the Harvard Divinity School on July 15, 1838.

9. Elton Trueblood, *The Life We Prize* (Waco: Word Books, 1951), 125.

10. François Fénelon, *The Seeking Heart* (Auburn: Seedsowers, 1699, 1982), 33.

11. Elisabeth Elliot, *Discipline: The Glad Surrender* (Old Tappan: Fleming H. Revell Company, 1982).

CHAPTER 5

1. Col. Larry R. Donnithorne (Ret.), *The West Point Way of Leadership* (New York: Currency Doubleday, 1993), 19ff.

2. Alicia Britt Chole, *Anonymous: Jesus' Hidden Years…and Yours* (Nashville: Integrity Publishers, 2006), 5.

3. Ibid., 61.

CHAPTER 6

1. Emory A. Griffin, *The Mind Changers: The Art of Christian Persuasion* (Wheaton: Tyndale House Publishers, 1976), 213ff.

2. Bob Benson, *Laughter in the Walls* (Alexandria: Gaither Family Resources, 1996), 6.

CHAPTER 7

1. Parker J. Palmer, *A Hidden Wholeness: The Journey Toward an Undivided Life* (San Francisco: Jossey-Bass, 2004).

2. J. I. Packer, *Knowing God* (Downers Grove, IL: Intervarsity Press, 1993).

3. Richard J. Foster, *Celebration of Discipline* (San Francisco: Harper Collins Publishers, 1978).

4. Henri J. M. Nouwen, *The Wounded Healer* (New York: Doubleday, 1972).

5. John Piper, *Desiring God: Meditations of a Christian Hedonist* (Portland: Multnomah Press, 1986).

6. Gordon MacDonald, *Ordering Your Private World* (Nashville: Thomas Nelson, 1984, 1985).

7. Elton Trueblood, *The Company of the Committed* (San Francisco: Harper & Row Publishers, 1961, 1980).

8. Leonard Sweet, *I Am a Follower: The Way, Truth, and Life of Following Jesus* (Nashville: Thomas Nelson, 2012).

9. Dr. James O. Davis, *How to Make Your Net Work: Tying Relational Knots for Global Impact* (Orlando: Cutting Edge International, 2013).

10. John C. Maxwell, *The 21 Irrefutable Laws of Leadership: Follow Them and People Will Follow You* (Nashville: Thomas Nelson Publishers, 1998).

11. Henri J. M. Nouwen, *In the Name of Jesus: Reflections on Christian Leadership* (New York: The Crossword Publishing Company, 1992), 48.

12. Elton Trueblood, *The Best of Elton Trueblood: An Anthology* (Nashville: Impact Books, 1979), 59.

13. Parker J. Palmer, *The Active Life: A Spirituality of Work, Creativity, and Caring* (San Francisco: Harper & Row Publishers, 1990).

14. Robert Lawrence Smith, *A Quaker Book of Wisdom* (New York: Eagle Brook, 1998), 1.

15. St. John of the Cross, trans. And ed. By E. Allison Peers, *Dark Night of the Soul* (New York: Image Books Doubleday, 1959).

16. Foster, *Celebration of Discipline*, 1.

17. Keith Miller, *The Becomers* (Waco: Word Books Publishing, 1973).

18. Mark Batterson, *The Circle Maker* (Grand Rapids: Zondervan, 2011).

19. Terry Muck, Dan Pawley, and Paul Robbins, "The Story of Raising a Pastoral Family" in *Leadership*, (Fall 1981).

CHAPTER 8

1. Nikos Kazantzakis, *Zorba, The Greek* (New York: Simon & Schuster, 1952).

2. Alfred Edersheim, *The Life and Times of Jesus the Messiah* (Peabody: Hendrickson Publishers, 1883), 255.

3. Mark Noll, *The Scandal of the Evangelical Mind* (Grand Rapids: William B. Eerdmans Publishing Company, 1994), 33ff.

4. Mortimer Adler & Charles van Doren, *How to Read a Book* (New York: Touchstone, 1972).

5. Donald B. Kraybill, *The Upside-Down Kingdom* (Scottsdale: Herald Press, 1978).

6. Alexandre Dumas, *The Count of Monte Cristo* (New York: Bantam Pathfinder Editions, 1936, 1963).

7. Robert D. Enright, "The Forgiveness Factor" in *Christianity Today*, January 10, 2000.

8. Laura Hillenbrand, *Unbroken: A World War II Story of Survival, Resilience, and Redemption* (New York: Random House, 2010).

9. Edmund Hillary, *High Adventure: The True Story of The First Ascent of Everest* (London: Hodder and Stoughton, 1955).

CHAPTER 9

1. Philip Yancey, *Where Is God When It Hurts?* (Grand Rapids: Zondervan, 1977).

2. Philip Yancey, *The Question That Never Goes Away* (Grand Rapids: Zondervan, 2013).

3. Nancy Guthrie, *Be Still My Soul: Embracing God's Purpose and Provision in Suffering: 25 Classic and Contemporary Readings on the Problem of Pain* (Wheaton: Crossway, 2010), 33.

4. Jerry Sittser, *A Grace Disguised: How the Soul Grows Through Loss* (Grand Rapids: Zondervan, 1998, 2004).

5. Viktor Frankl, *Man's Search for Meaning* (New York: Washington Square Press, 1946, 1984).

6. Thomas Merton, *New Seeds of Contemplation* (New York: Penguin Books, 1962, 1972), 161.

CHAPTER 10

1. Words and music written by Esther Kerr Rustthoi (1909-1962), published in *Singspiration*, 1941.

CONCLUSION

1. Lee Bolman and Terrence Deal, *Leading with Soul* (San Francisco: Jossey-Bass Publishers, 1995), 170.

2. Bob Benson, *Laughter in the Walls*, 24.

About the Author

Don Meyer is the president of the University of Valley Forge (UVF) and has been serving in that capacity since January 1, 1997. Meyer began his academic journey at Evangel University, formerly Central Bible College, in Springfield, Missouri, where he earned a bachelor's degree. He went on to earn a master's degree at Wheaton Graduate School in Wheaton, Illinois, and his doctorate at the University of Minnesota in Minneapolis, Minnesota. Meyer served for twenty-one years at North Central University, formerly North Central Bible College (NCBC), as a faculty member (three years) and as vice president of academic affairs (eighteen years).

Prior to accepting the position at NCBC, Meyer, an ordained Assemblies of God minister, pastored for seven years in Pennsylvania. He has spoken at camps, retreats, seminars and churches in the United States and overseas with extensive ministry in over twenty-five countries. He has contributed articles to various Christian publications and journals, and for over thirteen years has written a weekly column in the local newspaper of Phoenixville, Pennsylvania. His column, "Think About It," has been published in *Huffington Post*, *The Phoenix Reporter and Item*, and others. An archive of "Think About It" articles is available at www.valleyforge.edu/thinkaboutit.

Meyer is a native of Lebanon, Pennsylvania. He and his wife, Evie, married 48 years, live in Phoenixville. They have two sons, Darin and Kevin, and one grandson, Noah.

Meyer is a dynamic, insightful and well-known speaker and author who is available to speak at your event. If you are interested in exploring his participation in an upcoming event, please contact president@valleyforge.edu.

CONNECT WITH DON MEYER

Facebook: Facebook.com/DrDonMeyer
Twitter: @DrDonMeyer
Instagram: @DrDonMeyer